Praise for *How to Make Love (the Agape kind) with Jesus*

"Bil Aulenbach demonstrates how agape love enables the spirit of resurrection in the lives of people around us, when people who have been destroyed come back and overcome the forces that destroyed them."

> —Rev. Ken Wyant, retired UCC pastor, Biblical scholar, and member of Irvine United Congregational Church

"This little book explores the essential concept of agape love and its relationship to self, life, and spirituality. It may even create an opportunity for the thoughts and religious teachings you follow to be a source of further inquiry and investigation. This level of critical thinking is something each person and our world would greatly benefit from as we navigate the uncharted waters of the future."

> —Gretchen Cawley, MA, child care director

"Christianity has become Cross-Tianity, and this book does not require that you leave your brain outside. Traditional Christianity no longer works and is not reflective of the teachings of the historical Jesus."

> —Dr. Eduardo Jesús Arismendi-Pardi, Professor Emeritus of Mathematics; seminarian/MDiv student, International Theological Seminary; and member of UCC Abundant Peace Church

"In my midnineties, I find myself in a continual search for God in a scientific world. This book gives us a road map for continuing to grow in our own personal spiritual journey and also contains exciting ideas for the future of the institutional church."

> —Joan Thompson, MA, retired senior center director

How To

Make Love

(The Agape kind)

with Jesus

William Aulenbach,
MDiv, MSW, PhD

Quantity sales. Special discounts are available on quantity purchases by corporations, associations, and others. For details, contact the "Special Sales Department" at the address above.

Orders by US trade bookstores and wholesalers. Please contact BCH: (800) 431-1579 or visit www.bookch.com for details.

Printed in the United States of America

Cataloging-in-Publication Data

Names: Aulenbach, William, author.
Title: How to make love (the Agape kind) with Jesus / William Aulenbach, MDiv, MSW, PhD.
Description: Includes index. | Tustin, CA: Summit Run Press, 2023.
Identifiers: LCCN: 2023911529 | ISBN: 978-0-9986789-0-8 (paperback) | 978-0-9986789-1-5 (ebook)
Subjects: LCSH Jesus Christ--Example. | Agapé. | Love--Religious aspects--Christianity. | BISAC RELIGION / Christianity / General
Classification: LCC BV4639 .A85 2023 | DDC 241/.4--dc23

First Edition

27 26 25 24 23   10 9 8 7 6 5 4 3 2 1

NoOneUpThere

Rev. David Keighley

A wise, eighty-five-year-old priest once told me, "There's NoOneUpThere."
Strange comment for a priest, I thought,
Even for an American Episcopalian one.
A fire engine had hit him and his friend on their motorcycles.
His friend was killed outright.
NoOneUpThere didn't stop it happening.

"If NoOneUpThere was letting such hideous things like this happen," he
    said, "I want no part of this religion."
"Worship NoOneUpThere? No way."
So I wondered . . .
Why didn't NoOneUpThere keep my mum alive; stop her cancer; zap her
    cells?
Why did NoOneUpThere let Susan and Joe suffer the loss of their baby
    Lucy?
Why did NoOneUpThere, all-powerful creator of the Universe,
    send a tsunami to that exquisite sandy beach?
Why did NoOneUpThere of our faith, let the terrorist with his faith, kill and
    maim in our lovely cities?
NoOneUpThere's Omnipotence seems to fall short.

Does NoOneUpThere pick and choose I wonder?
You pray for the tornado to miss your village, but what about the one it hits?
You pray for Mike to get safely home tonight on the foggy motorway,
    but what of the deaths in that multiple pile-up?
Did their prayers to NoOneUpThere not work as well as yours?
Whose side is NoOneUpThere on in war?
Did NoOneUpThere hear Hitler's prayers for victory, and ignore them?

Did we create NoOneUpThere, I wonder, through fear and wonder?
With the first few words uttered by frightened cave dwellers gazing at the
      miracle of a rising sun after the darkness.
We're told if horses had a God it would be a horse.
"Our Father who art in NoHeavenUpThere . . ."
NoOneUpThere looking down, taking care, making things better.
Just us, made in the image of NoOneUpThere but doing his job just the
      same.
Loving, caring, healing.

My wise priestly friend now uses the word "Creation" for NoOneUpThere.
A force for good everywhere in the Universe.
No gender. No judging. No son to send.
Still creating. Still evolving. Tsunami and tornado. Just Being Creation.
"I am in you and you are in me and I and my father are one" said Jesus,
      maybe.
Perhaps he also agrees there's NoOneUpThere.
Just the force of creation and the power of Jesus in us all.
But Down Here, Now!

(Dedicated to Rev. Dr. Bil Aulenbach)

From David John Keighley, *Poems, Piety, and Psyche: Progressive Poems for Rebellious Christians* (Eugene, OR: Resource Publications, 2020), 33–34. Printed with permission.

CONTENTS

PREFACE

God is the same as nature.

—Sister Julian of Norwich

A six-year-old girl stood in front of her parents and emphatically stated, "Why should I outgrow my invisible friend? Isn't God your invisible friend?" (Why is this six-year-old so right?)

To live life to the fullest, one has to keep evolving, even at ninety years old. For me, evolving means questioning, changing, growing, and transforming.

My evolving life began in 1932 under the tutelage of my dad, "Ham" (Hamilton), an Episcopal priest, and my mom, "Saint" Pearl.

I was a great Episcopalian, as was Jesus—so I thought.

In 1950, I went to college. This was my first transformation. I became my own person, no longer Ham's little boy. While there, I divorced God, Jesus, and the Episcopal church and married "St. Cerveza."

After college, I was commissioned in the Marine Corps (my second transformation), where I found foxhole religion. After serving for three years, I felt that I would rather love people than kill them. (But it was and still is an honor to have served our great country.)

So I went to seminary, where I had my third transforming experience, the start of my spiritual (meaning "authentic") journey in life.

I had my fourth transformation while in seminary. Riding on my motorcycle, I was broadsided by a fire engine. My best friend was killed in the accident, which left me asking, "Why? Where was God?"

I found that answer: She had nothing to do with the accident. Free will did. (God did not tell me to buy that murdercycle.)

The church might not like that answer because its leaders keep inferring that God is running the earth (or is it now the universe?), God is directly involved in our lives (She "planned" the accident), and God's "Son" died for our sins. Ugh!

No way did I want to tell the church that the theology about some master puppeteer god who lived above the flat earth in a mansion made no sense today. So quietly I started calling God "Creation." No one has called me on that yet.

Then I met and married a wonderful woman and had my fifth transformation. I had been a bachelor for twenty-eight years and now had to learn to be one with my Annie while each of us still maintained our individuality. This has been hard work but most rewarding. We celebrated our sixty-second anniversary in June 2023, and she is still my beautiful best friend.

Our second daughter (born in 1965), a rubella baby, was multichallenged. This was my sixth transforming experience. Annie and I were not at all ready for this challenge, but together, we grew in the faith, became a stronger team, and worked extremely hard to teach her to be independent, which she is. Today she lives and works in Seattle.

As my ministry progressed, I was able to do what Jesus asked me to do, "love the least of these" (Matt. 25:40), and had fantastic ministries.

In 1969, very loudly I stated, "The war in Vietnam is wrong." The church, where I had a youth ministry involving 2,500 young people, fired me—for being against war. I'm still processing that.

Being fired was my seventh transformation. My faith sustained me, and I kept moving forward, trying to build the Kin-dom (our faith is about real people, kin, not kings) of love in Hawai'i with all sorts of exciting projects.

In 1975, we moved to Southern California for better educational opportunities for our differently abled but bright ten-year-old daughter.

However, the Episcopal Diocese in Los Angeles was not welcoming. I suspect that I was too progressive. I fought for ordaining women clergy, supporting equality for the LGBTQUI community, remarrying divorced people, constantly updating *The Book of Common Prayer*, looking at the Bible through Jewish eyes, redefining God, rediscovering the historical Jesus, changing the role of seminaries, redesigning the institutional church, and standing up against fundamentalism as well as bad government, to name a few items on my agenda.

For the past forty-seven years, while working in secular fields, I have been actively involved in semi progressive churches either as a poorly paid assistant or volunteer.

After I was fired again (1988) by an incompetent priest (he was fired six months later), Annie and I became members of "St. Mattress," staying in bed on Sunday mornings. Although we missed being members of an agape-centered community, this independence allowed me to be totally honest about my beliefs, doubts, faith, and growth and to expose the roadblocks preventing the institutional church from being all it can be.

In 2008, a clergy friend (a United Church of Christ pastor) asked me where we were going to church. He laughed when I said, "St. Mattress" then responded, "When you have too many bedsores, take a look at Irvine United Congregational Church." We did and I had another transformation: an Episcopal priest becoming a member of a UCC congregation in the company of other progressive retired clergy who were Lutheran, Disciples of Christ, Methodist, Presbyterian and even Southern Baptist. The pastor at that time, the Reverend Dr. Paul Tellström, was most welcoming and became a good friend. He retired in 2019.

I have had a rich and full ministry here, all as a volunteer, in the midst of a diverse, accepting, and socially active group of Followers. I have continued evolving here as I share the message that Jesus was about agape, the highest form of love.

My most radical and probably impossible project: replace the gruesome symbol of Christianity, a torturous cross, with a dove, a symbol of love and peace.

My hope is that you are interested in changing and evolving in your life. In order to change, we need to know where we came from, what we were originally taught (in religious school or by our parents and teachers), whether it is still applicable today, and what new directions we might want to follow. So let's start at the beginning.

Peace Love Joy Hope
Bil

POSTSCRIPT

I wrote my first book, *Let Us Pray*, in 1985.

My second book, *How to Get to Heaven without Going to Church*, was written in 1997 and was really the start of my Progressive Christianity journey.

My third book, *What's Love Got to Do with It? "Everything," Says Jesus*, was written in 2008.

My fourth book, *Cramming for the Finals*, was written in 2017.

I think too many Christian churches would rather die than change! But however my books were written, edited, or accepted, the series shows my growth as a Progressive. This book, once again, shows my development into Progressive Christianity.

In the workbook (at the back of this book), I list suggested readings at the end of every chapter to help you with your own spiritual growth.

INTRODUCTION

WHERE DO WE START?

All Christians should be heretics.
—Rev. David Keighley, *Poems, Piety, and Psyche*

I think the number one problem with our society is that no one will assume responsibility for anything!
But please don't quote me!

Do you want to look deeper into your faith? It can be scary, like any change. Remember going from middle school or junior high to senior high school? Lots of unknowns. Apprehension. "Can I do it? Do I want to do it?" This is similar. The best thing is that you can find folks who will help you through. Remember, this is a gradual process. You won't be graded, but it is important for you to define where you are now. Sometimes you have to take a statement that interests you and simply play with it in your mind before you make any decisions. You have to feel free to ask questions, have doubts. This is the most important part of growing.

A PRIMARY BELIEF FOUNDATION

Who was Jesus? What was his message? Was it that he "undeaded" or conquered death? Or "He died for our sins?" Maybe it was about his magic tricks or the Golden Rule? Perhaps it was about agape, unconditional love. Do you have another idea?

I suspect most Christians would say, "Jesus died on a cross for our sins."

I was never much for the idea that a Jewish peasant from Galilee "undeaded" for my mess-ups so that I do not have to be responsible. I see the Easter stories very differently.

My answer is that Jesus was about agape. *Please feel free to quote me this time.* It has taken many years for me to arrive at this point, but it has also added a new dimension to my life.

The first step in explaining my belief will be to review the process of evolving and its key components, especially as it concerns our faith. Next, we will need to dehumanize God and rehumanize Jesus so that we can experience some new revelations about who the human Jesus was and what he did.

The institutional church might not be happy about this because almost all the dogma, doctrine, and tradition of the historical church will disappear. However, what will emerge is a rich, fulfilling, life-changing transformation.

Today I have so many new tools in my theological toolkit than did my dad (Episcopal clergy) or the church of my youth than I did or even while in seminary. Let us look at these tools.

The list starts with all the technology at my fingertips, which brings new information right to my desk.

Next is all the new material found in the Dead Sea Scrolls, the Nag Hammadi Library in Egypt, and other ancient libraries.

We cannot forget advanced archaeology techniques or the scholars who are able to look at new information without ecclesiastical biases because they are scholars, not ordained clergy.

The exploration of space has been very important because the findings have helped put the universe and my theology into a new perspective.

Interfaith cooperation has been a plus. Muslims, Jews, Sikhs, Buddhists, Hindus, and others have also discovered that we are all dealing with humanity and its challenges, which has helped make interfaith cooperation a must. Thank you to Pope John XXIII (1881–1963) and his ecumenical encyclical (a papal letter).

The most important thing to remember with all this newness is that the primary message of Jesus *never* gets old. The Great Commandment, from the Old Testament, about loving self, neighbor, and Creation (Matt. 22:37–38) is incredibly old but will be relevant as long as there are people.

THE PROCESS OF EVOLVING

I know the universe around me is evolving and constantly changing to a different state or condition. My body, face, and brain are vastly different than they were forty, sixty, or eighty years ago. I am evolving into an old man, whether I want to or not.

But humans do have a choice as to whether we want our thinking to get old or to evolve. Too many folks have no interest in evolving because it demands change, sometimes producing pain or discomfort.

A good friend of mine had no interest in changing his theology and would admit that it was still at an early Sunday school level, but he claimed it worked for him. Every time I wrote a new book or paper, he would remind me that he had no interest in reading it because his mind was made up and he did not want to be confused with the facts. This was always friendly banter and I appreciated that he was open about his opinion. Many people are not. But I felt sorry that he had this approach to living.

Following are the necessary traits one must possess if one wants to evolve.

Desire to Evolve

The first attribute is wanting to evolve or change. Personally, I love change. That is how I grow, regardless of my age. I want my mind to be challenged with new ideas. In the 1980s, the computer became an important household tool. I decided I wanted to learn to use it, as challenging as it was. As the complexity of the computer world evolves, I try to stay current, but it is not easy.

I have friends who refused to learn computer skills when they had the chance: it was too challenging. Unfortunately, thirty years later they feel left out. For example, the COVID vaccination opportunity was highly dependent on having computer skills, and without them it was next to impossible to figure out how to schedule a vaccination.

Ability to Think

The second ingredient in evolving is knowing how to think. I can hear some of you saying, "But everyone knows how to think." Not really. If you live in a Communist country or a dictatorship, you can think only what the leader wants you to think. Maybe you work for a company that simply wants you to do what you're told. In the Roman Catholic and fundamentalist churches, members are discouraged from thinking on their own. If you do, you will be asked to leave. In my Episcopal church, which some consider liberal, the leaders allow me to think only so much before I have to stop or lie or leave.

For example, if I were to tell my bishop that I am an A-theist (I do not believe in a humanlike god UpThere), he would either defrock me or suggest I transfer my membership to a Unity-Unitarian church. I do not think most of the Episcopal bishops appreciate my referring to their God as NoOneUpThere or suggesting that god is a man-made concept.

Interest in Listening

Third, evolving demands the art of listening. Good listening is a skill that's not easy to master because we are often busy getting ready to say what we want to say. We interrupt, yell, throw in a put-down, and sometimes walk away, especially if we disagree.

3

Let me share an example. For fifty-plus years I put the Gospel of John in the "Useless" file. John made next to no sense to me. (I had closed my mind. Bad idea!) Then in 2018, I was in a Bible study class reading that gospel. I let everyone know my disdain for the gospel, but the leader, the Reverend Ken Wyant, a retired UCC pastor, started making sense about the power of that gospel. For a change, I listened, and now I see John as a powerful ally for demonstrating that Jesus was about agape, not resurrection fairy tales, all because I listened.

Are you willing to concentrate on listening to new ideas? Listening does not mean you have to accept the ideas. It simply means you have to hear the presenter in total. Listening is not as easy as one might think.

Desire to Transform Oneself

The final step in evolving has to do with the desire to transform one's life. Not everyone wants to transform. I know lots of people who love to hate, hang on to their anger, insist on not forgiving, want their pound of flesh, have to have their own way, want to be homeless, and refuse to change.

Some folks think their lives are fine. Others seem to be on a quest to be all they can be. I know I use only about 10 percent of my brain. I would love to use just 2 percent more. Maybe I should take a course in Koine Greek (New Testament Greek) or add five minutes more of walking to our daily schedule. I just finished a course entitled "Preaching and the Future Church." Even at ninety years old, I want to transform my preaching.

This book is about changing, growing, transforming, and evolving.

I invite you to come along.

WHAT DO ALL THOSE WORDS MEAN?

In the process of growing, you need to know the meanings of words. Faith is built on beliefs, and words explain beliefs. It's time to increase your church vocabulary. Not only are you going to see some outrageous definitions of churchy words, but you will also have an opportunity to see how the meanings of these words have changed throughout my life. As you read the words, think about how you would have defined them a while ago and how you would describe them now.

I have provided definitions based on four periods in my life:

Ages 1–24: Preseminary
Ages 24–27 and 27–53: Seminary (huge changes) and postseminary
Ages 54–75: Mature
Ages 76–90+: Golden

agape (a-gah-peh)

1–24: I had never heard the word.

24–53: I'd heard the word but never understood its power.

54–75: This is Jesus's message.

76–90+: This is the most important word in the world.

Agape has unbelievable transforming powers. It's the highest form of love because it (1) is unconditional; (2) accepts everyone, no matter where a person is in life's journey; (3) always forgives, almost instantaneously; and (4) cares, at the deepest level, for every human being.

Agape is easy to say, but living it takes a lifetime of practicing.

god, GOD, or God

1–24: He is like Santa Claus but meaner.

24–53: God is out, Creation is in.

54–75: I became an A-theist, anti-SomeOneUpThere.

76–90+: So many different ideas exist.

Bottom line: no one truly knows. Most religions will tell you they do know because they have configured (invented) one to fulfill their needs.

Neanderthals are believed to have invented a god to help them hunt better. Christians designed one to support their idea that God's son died on a cross—for all of us. (That thinking plays havoc with the idea that we must grow up and be responsible for ourselves. Ask Sigmund Freud, who thinks religion keeps us infantile.)

So I call god/GOD/God "Creation," a word that is not anthropomorphic, has no gender, and encompasses the entire universe, which is so big that it is beyond most folks' imagination.

I used to say, "God is love." Then I realized I was telling you that I knew who God was. I don't.

So now I say, "Love (agape) is God," I am sharing with you what is really important to me and my concept of Creation.

Jesus

1–24: He was God and could do anything.

24–53: He was sort of a man-God.

54–75: He was a historical Jewish man who gave us the key to living life to the fullest.

76–90+: He was a Jewish man who lived in the region of Galilee from about 6 BCE to 30 or 33 CE and had a straightforward message about agape and transformation that changed, and still is changing, the course of individuals as well as the world.

He has been accused of being everything from God to a criminal. He was executed by the Romans for sedition, claiming to be a king, who he never was nor claimed to be.

Christ/christ

1–24: This is Jesus's last name or the second part of a cuss word.

24–53: This is an adjective describing who I think Jesus is.

54–75: Everyone has one. A clergy friend used to say, sort of kidding, "Show me your checkbook, and I'll tell you who your christ is." My definition: that to which every human being turns to try to make life fulfilling. Examples include money, power, prestige, drugs, sex, another person, and a fantasy—for starters.

76–90+: My Christ/christ is the Jewish Jesus, a fellow human being.

Holy Spirit

1–24: It is like a Halloween ghost.

24–53: It is part of the Trinity, but I do not understand the thinking behind the Trinity.

54–75: It is the spirit of agape that lives within every human being. But people have to decide whether they want that spirit to be part of their lives or not. Too many do not.

76–90+: Everyone is born with this spirit of agape. Unfortunately, one's environment can suppress this spirit, but it is always there and always ready to transform us.

When folks allow the "HS" (part of agape) to direct their lives, it is transforming.

Bible

1–24: It is a big boring book that is holy/sacred. I never read it, but people read it to us in church. Almost always, it was boring.

24–53: This is a fascinating religious history of Judaism and then Christianity before it was Christianity. It takes a lifetime of study to even start to understand it.

54–75: Because I am not a Jew, I do not fully understand it but need to keep trying to do so. It is best read "through Jewish eyes."

76–90+: I read it daily and find new truths.

The Bible is a collection of some sixty-seven (depending on which version) different writings by men, mostly Jewish, who wanted to share their understanding of their Higher Power. It is composed of universal truths, lies, contradictions, gross exaggerations, pithy sayings, inspiring words, hatred, violence, love, romance, and more.

It is a bestseller that very few people have read from beginning to end, if at all. It can be boring and act as a cure for insomnia.

One can twist much of it to substantiate one's point of view, good or evil.

It is divided into three parts—Old Testament, New Testament, and Apocrypha—and at least some portion of the Bible has been translated into 3,415 languages. How is that for the possibility of errors?

The Old Testament was originally written in Hebrew, but in Jesus's time it had been translated into Greek. The New Testament was written in either Aramaic (street Hebrew) or Greek (not classical). Today you can find over fifty English versions of the Bible. No wonder there is so much confusion about what it says.

It's a religious history book that is *never* to be taken literally or accepted as accurate history. (See *midrash*.)

midrash

1–24: Huh?

24–53: Huh?

54–75: This is probably the most important process one can use to understand the Bible and what the story inside the story truly means.

76–90+: This is a Hebrew word meaning "biblical interpretation."

Every story in the Bible needs to go through the midrash process when we read it. Most stories are not historical accounts but fabricated tales wrapped around a truth. This is a Jewish approach to sharing truths. For example, the parable of Jesus walking on water, an impossibility, is really about the storms in life we all face, but by using the tools of agape, we too can figuratively "walk on water" and calm any storm. Ask me. (See Mark 6:45–52).

"Saint" Paul

1–24: Boring!

24–53: He was an extremely complex Jewish rabbi who had a lot to say. I thought I liked him in seminary, but the more I learned about him, the less I liked him.

54–75: On further thought, I almost always disagree with his thinking.

76–90+: He was born a Jew and died a Jew. He was a well-trained Pharisee who started out persecuting Followers of the Way (Jesus's friends) but ended up being a Follower, much to the consternation of the Jewish hierarchy and some Followers of Jesus.

Paul never met nor heard Jesus. He never heard the word *Christian* nor had any idea what it meant. He wasn't one, ever.

Paul made up stuff about Jesus that had no basis in reality—and many Followers bought it and still do. I don't! For example, his claim that Jesus is the "sacrificial lamb" is, for me, a silly, offensive fairy tale.

Paul's writings need to be categorized in the history books as obsolete. Humanity has evolved vastly in the last two thousand years. Paul's silliness hasn't. Let's let him and his strange thinking go so Followers can evolve.

Some think Paul was gay, but I couldn't care less. I just want to put him and his stories in the past.

Nativity stories

1–24: I loved the story of Jesus's birth (I had no idea there were three different ones), the Christmas season, and all its trappings—especially the presents. My dad's church made a huge deal out of the story, as do most Christian churches.

24–53: The Christmas season is always difficult for clergy. With so many services, sermons, pageants, parties, and activities the magic came out of it years ago.

54–75: I now know three Christmas stories: one in Matthew, one in Luke, and a made-up one that combines the other two and adds some extraneous details. When I retired, I stopped going to Christmas services because they had little to do with what the church should be about.

76–90+: Two official tales are told in the New Testament, and they are as different as day and night. Neither is true. Both were created some sixty-plus years after Jesus died. They served two purposes: (1) they made God responsible for the birth of Jesus rather than the Roman soldier who raped Mary (see explanation on page 32), and (2) Matthew and Luke wanted to make sure that Jesus's birth was recognized by humble shepherds, wise men from afar, heavenly hosts, and a brilliant star.

In 333 CE, the Roman emperor Constantine decided to set aside December 25 (then thought to be the shortest day of the year and an occasion for wild celebrations) as the birthday of Jesus, even though logic defies that idea. Unfortunately, folks in the business world have taken over Christmas, so too much of it is about commercialism and that is fine with me.

I enjoy the secular Christmas but agree with the Eastern Orthodox Church, which ignores December 25 and celebrates January 6, Epiphany, or the manifestation of the baby Jesus, who was born of a woman and grew into a man, to the gentiles. I hope the business folks do not try to hijack Epiphany too.

virgin births

1–24: God can do anything He wants.

24–53: How do I explain virgin births to my junior high youth?

54–75: It's impossible. How did that fairy tale start? (See *midrash*.)

76–90+: Impossible, especially since the Aramaic word used to describe Mary means "young woman." It was simply the translation into Greek that made her a "virgin."

I could not care less whether Mary's hymen was intact or not. She is not my Christ.

Resurrection

1–24: Wow! Dead people can come alive.

24–53: How do I explain a dead man undeading, walking through doors, and scaring people? This idea does not sit well with me, but as a clergyperson I have to market it.

54–75: These stories are not history. They are powerful metaphors.

76–90+: Dead people undeading can happen only in fantasy land, Greek mythology, Christian churches, and the minds of people who refuse to accept that these stories are metaphors, invented about sixty years after Jesus died. Literal resurrections are preposterous, but this idea is not: all of us have our "Good (really bad) Fridays," but through the teaching of Jesus and agape, we can resurrect or transform them into "Easters."

Ask the prodigal son—or me.

dogma, doctrine, and tradition

1–24: Who cares? They have too many long, hard words.

24–53: Yikes. There is a lot. Maybe people will think I'm smart if I use all those big words and say them correctly.

54–75: Who cares? They are all made-up stuff that detracts from Jesus's primary message.

76–90+: If one accepts God as Creation and Jesus (my Christ) as a fellow traveler, sage, and revolutionary, all dogma, doctrine, and tradition become ancient history.

miracles

1–24: Anyone who could do magic like that had to be God or at least related.

24–53: Miracles taken literally sure confuse the message of Jesus. Maybe I need to look further into them.

54–75: They have great truths inside their sometimes preposterous stories.

76–90+: "A little story with a big meaning" was what my Sunday school teacher told me about the parables and miracle stories. I have always liked that idea. If one reads them as the literal truth, they all sound like fairy tales. If one reads them like "a little story," then they possess life-changing truths.

life after death

1–24: I am going to live forever (even though that isn't possible) because a church said one of my gifts at baptism is eternal (which nothing is) life.

24–53: I have to spend a great deal of time and attention in my ministry dealing with this issue. What do I really believe?

54–75: There is nothing after this life, so live every day to its fullest.

76–90+: Thanks to science, modern medicine, and reality, I do not see anything after this life, no matter how hard people try to convince me otherwise. Science tells me that four minutes after my brain shuts off, I start decomposing.

My life has been rich and fulfilling. What else could I want? It is certainly not to live in eternity with some of my least favorite people.

church versus Church

1–24: Huh?

24–53: There's a huge difference.

54–75: There is a tremendous gap between the two.

76–90+: The *church*, in my books, is the institution of organized religion, which can be cultish, is big business, is power hungry, and is often diametrically opposed to Jesus's message of unconditional love. On the other hand, the *Church* is made up of those Believers who recognize Jesus as their Christ and live agape. It has no theology, buildings, traditions, dogma, doctrine, liturgies, or hierarchy.

I could define plenty of other churchy words, but this is enough for now.

Where Do We Start?

You are about to enter the heart of this book, the foundation stone of Progressive Christianity and the world-changing message of Jesus.

In the Gospels, Jesus is asked 182 questions. He answers maybe 8 of them.
He himself asks 307. Maybe faith isn't about certainty, but learning
to ask—and to sit in the complexity of—good questions.
—Kevin Nye

CHAPTER 1

UNDERSTANDING AGAPE

My little ones, let's not talk about love. Let's put love into action and make it real.
—1 John 3:18 (*Cotton Patch Gospel*)

It was Christmas morning and Dad was reading his four-year-old the Nativity story. When his son asked, "What's a stable?" Dad thought for a moment and then put his definition into terms his son could relate to: "It's like your brother's room without a stereo."

You have heard and maybe believe that Jesus arose from the dead, he died for our sins, and he is the Son of God plus. Now you are going to read new ideas that might contradict the old. This could make you feel uncomfortable, maybe guilty because the ideas go against what your family believes, or fearful of going to hell. You may be able to change those past ideas by simply opening your mind to a new one. You are going to learn about the Greek word *agape*, and you just need to understand it as a concept. At some point, you will read that Jesus wasn't about dying for your sins but was much more about practicing the concept of agape. If it makes sense, keep reading. If it doesn't make sense, keep reading. There is more to it.

First, let's try to understand the term *agape*. The quick translation of that word is "love," but I need to explain it in a more relatable way, like Dad did with the word *stable*. The English language has only one word for love, and it is used for a large variety of different subjects. People talk about loving their cars, ice cream, wine, a movie, their significant other, or their pet, but no one else really understands the intensity of feeling that their use of the word *love* implies. I hope there is a great deal of difference between loving ice cream and loving your significant other.

Unfortunately, no one but the speaker knows that intensity. Some people have told me that they loved their spouse, but their dog gave them what they wanted, unconditional love. Their spouse gave them love with all kinds of conditions.

The major language of the New Testament writings was Greek, although a few manuscripts were written in Aramaic. For our study of the word *love*, we will look at the Greek language.

TYPES OF LOVE

Greek has four different words for love, each signifying a different meaning and intensity.

Philia

Love at its lowest intensity is *philia*, an emotion that exists between friends, between people at work, and even toward things. Several cities are called Philadelphia, which translates into "the city of brotherly love." Philia is probably closer to the idea of "like" than love. It demands little other than acknowledgment, a certain level of caring, and a minimal amount of emotional involvement.

Storge

The next level of love is called *storge*. It is the affection among siblings and parents and perhaps relatives or close friends. Maybe you do not even like a certain family member, but if anyone says or does anything negative to that person, you rise to his or her defense. This is storge love, which demands something in return, usually loyalty.

Let me try an example close to home. Our middle daughter was a rubella (German measles) baby, resulting in her being deaf and legally blind, as well as having many other issues. At the age of thirty-two, she walked into a moving car because she did not see it. She was in a coma for two weeks, and when she came out of it, she had to learn how to walk, talk, sign, eat, and do life all over. The damage was so severe that it affected her organizational skills, her ability to follow through, and some of her social and people skills. She became a different person. Our other two daughters now have made it their job to help steer her through life. This is not always an easy task, but it is something storge love does.

Eros

The next love word is *eros*, or erotic love involving our sensual/sexual being. This love exists mostly between two people who are committed to each other. It is a much deeper love than the above two. It ties deeply into our emotions and very definitely demands something in return.

Anne and I have been married for sixty-two years. She is my eros and still my best friend. I have had strong sensual/sexual feelings for her since our first date. We have a great time doing life together. I still find her beautiful, wrinkles and all. There has been lots of genuine forgiveness over the years, so neither of us carries negative baggage. I have never loved someone as much as I love her, but eros still demands that she love me. If she didn't, we would need to go our separate ways.

Agape

The fourth word for love in the Greek language is *agape*. It demands nothing in return and is given freely with no strings attached. It cannot be earned, purchased, pleaded for, or cajoled. It is simply given. *Agape* is the word the writers used when Jesus spoke about love in the gospels (116 times). This kind of love is more difficult to achieve because as fallible human beings we almost always expect something in return, either directly or indirectly. Agape expects nothing.

For example, when I was in college, our family vacationed every year in a town off the southern New Jersey coastline. In my sophomore year in college, I became a lifeguard for the city of Stone Harbor, New Jersey. One day, I was alone on the lifeguard stand when I noticed a boy on his bicycle pedaling in the sand toward me. When he arrived, he was out of breath but managed to say, "Hey, mister, there's a little girl drowning down at Sixty-Seventh Street and there aren't any lifeguards around."

I knew Sixty-Seventh Street was not in our city, but I also knew that someone was drowning and that I needed to do something about it. I told the boy I was going to borrow his bike. I would blow my whistle and other lifeguards would come running. He should tell them about the little girl drowning on Sixty-Seventh Street. I told him they would drive him there so that he could pick up his bike.

When I approached on the bike, I saw a small crowd and asked where the little girl was. The people gathered there were Hispanic and spoke little English. They pointed to the ocean, conveyed that the girl was twelve and said, "No swim." I knew that she had been in the ocean for at least a half hour. Then, by gesturing, I told them that I would swim out in her direction.

After about fifteen minutes, I saw her. I could not believe she was still afloat. Finally, I got close enough to grab her, and soon the other lifeguards helped me bring in the little girl. The medics resuscitated her, and I was sure she was going to make it.

I went back to my station, where the captain of the lifeguards came over to me and sort of scolded me for doing a rescue in a city other than Stone Harbor.

I never thought of the story again because it was just one of the many rescues I had made over the years. Later, when I learned about agape, I remembered this story. It had all the elements of unconditional love. I did not know the girl and she did not know me. She was in a heap of trouble, and without a rescue she would have died. I, too, could have lost my life. I knew that I was not supposed to save people in Avalon but intuitively I knew I had to risk my life to save the girl's. This is agape, unconditional love—what I believe is the foundation stone of Jesus's ministry.

AGAPE DAD

Now let us look at a parable best known as "The Prodigal Son." I prefer to call it "The Father Who Showed Agape." It is found only in the Gospel of Luke 15:11–32.

It starts with the younger son, who talked his father into giving him his inheritance before he died. Quickly, the son spent it all on fast living. Penniless, he was then forced to live with the pigs and to eat their food.

Here comes agape, unconditional love, forgiveness, and caring. Dad saw him approaching in the distance, ran to him, hugged and kissed him, and ordered his servants to wrap him in the best robe, put a ring on his finger, and kill a fatted calf to celebrate his return. Never does the story suggest that the son received a tongue-lashing, punishment, or banishment. This is unconditional love. Here are Luke's words: "This son of mine was dead and has come back to life [this sounds a lot like Easter]; he was lost and is now found. And they started celebrating."

For many, this is the heart of the resurrection experience. All of us have been figuratively "dead" because of some horrendous experience. However, with the tools of agape, we can turn that into an Easter, a positive experience.

Jesus and this parable always push me to a higher plane, which demands that we accept all people, no matter where they are on their life's journey. There can be no exceptions or lists of unacceptables because Followers of Jesus accept everyone unconditionally, no matter what.

AGAPE IN ACTION

Another parable, "The Good Samaritan," found in Luke 10: 25–37, should be called "Agape in Action."

The story emphasizes two major themes about agape. The first is when a lawyer was testing Jesus and asked, "What must I do to inherit eternal life?"

Jesus told the story of a man, and we can only surmise he was Jewish, who was going from Jerusalem (2,600 feet high) down to Jericho when he was robbed, savagely beaten, stripped naked, and left to die. A Jewish priest (rabbi) and a Levite (important person in the Temple) passed by the man. However, a Samaritan man stopped, saw the Jewish man's horrible physical condition, bandaged his wounds, put him on his own animal, went to an inn, paid what amounted to two days' hotel costs, and promised to pay the innkeeper the rest of the bill when he returned. (Another Easter story?) The Samaritan had never met or seen this man before. Nor can we forget that Jews and Samaritans had hated each other for centuries and their tribes were bitter enemies. Despite these factors, this Samaritan demonstrated agape and directly and indirectly cared for his tribe's enemy.

Remember, Jesus demanded that we "love our enemies" (Luke 6:28). This story is about giving unconditional love with no strings attached, totally accepting (both giver and receiver), and showing agape to one's enemies. The caring aspect was way beyond all expectations. This is another great story about the power of agape.

I love the ending of this story, as Jesus asks the lawyer this question: "Which of these three do you think was the neighbor?" (as in "Love your neighbor as yourself"). The lawyer said, "The one who showed mercy." Jesus said to him (and to me and you), "Go and do likewise."

Is there any doubt that agape was Jesus's primary message? As a Follower, my job is to keep loving "the hell" (the negative) out of every human being. It has taken me many years to evolve to this place. Unfortunately, the church's idea that Jesus died for us rotten sinners was in the way of my seeing clearly what I now believe is obvious.

Now let's clarify some ideas so that you and I can have a better mutual understanding. These are ideas with a different twist, such as love versus like, tough love, indifference, conscience, and justice. You could discover a different way of looking at some important issues.

If your faith causes you to love fewer people instead of
more people, we're doing it wrong. . . . Because love wins.
—Unknown

CHAPTER 2

CLARIFICATIONS

Let all that you do be done in love.
—I Corinthians 16:14

This is a true exchange that took place in a courtroom.

    Attorney: What is the first thing your husband said to you that morning?

    Witness: He was waking up and asked, "Where am I, Cathy?"

    Attorney: Why did that upset you so much?

    Witness: I'm his wife and my name is Susan.

    A lawyer stood up to put [Jesus] to the test, saying, "Teacher, what shall I do to inherit eternal life?" He said to him, "What is written in the law? How do you read?" And he answered, "You shall love the Lord your God with all your heart, and with all your soul, and with all your strength, and with all your mind; and your neighbor as yourself." And Jesus said to him, "You have answered right; do this and you shall live" (Luke 10:25–28).

As demonstrated in the above court scene, it is important to understand my thinking about some concepts so we don't confuse "Cathy" with "Susan."

    Agape is not about liking everyone; it can include disliking people, but we have to forgive them and even care for them. It allows one to be tough if the end result is love. Sometimes people hide behind indifference because it can be sneaky. We simply need to learn to identify indifference and call it out. Also, we must never let our conscience be our guide, and we need to treat everyone justly. Agape covers all this.

The above paragraph includes five concepts I want to clarify because they are integral to moving forward: love versus like, tough love, indifference, conscience, and justice. People often misunderstand what these items mean, so let us look at them more closely.

AGAPE LOVE VERSUS LIKE

Until I went to seminary, I envisioned Jesus as Mr. Nice Guy. I am not saying that Jesus was *not* a nice guy most of the time, but I am emphasizing that at times he could be tough as nails. In seminary, I started seeing Jesus in an entirely different light. My thinking continued to evolve, and today, I see Jesus as a fellow human being with a powerful, transforming message.

Jesus seemed to be at odds, at least in the New Testament, with his religious leaders much of the time, especially when they were trying to entrap him. One has to know that Jesus was not very fond of the Romans (the oppressing occupiers), the Samaritans (bitter enemies of Jews for centuries), most gentiles, and people who gave him a hard time. But agape is not about liking; it is about loving unconditionally. So in his ministry, we see Jesus healing gentiles, helping Romans, dealing lovingly with the Samaritans, accepting tax collectors, healing lepers, and having positive interactions with people whom Jewish leaders considered unworthy.

My wife and I live in a senior community. Some people there are not so nice. They start nasty gossip, say awful things to and about other people, and sometimes do malicious things. I have been the recipient of some of these negative activities. There are people in this community I do not like. But if anyone asked me to help them, I would. This is my role as a Follower: to love people unconditionally even though I might not like them.

TOUGH LOVE

Tough love does not have a great deal of *like* in it. It is a love that confronts people with the truth, as painful as it might be, often followed by some sort of action perceived by the receiver as being negative. For example, let's consider an adult child who lives at home, with his parents, takes drugs, does not work, and is abusive to his parents or anyone who might question his behavior. The parents, exhausted by empty promises, tell their child to be out of the house in twenty-four hours and not to return until he is sober and in a program. If he tries to return, the parents will call the police, have him arrested, and leave him in jail. This is tough love, and sometimes it is tougher on the giver than the receiver.

Often the role of tough love is to push a person into his or her "gutter," a place where the destructive behavior is no longer bearable to the person and he or she becomes willing to seek help. This is not an easy role, but it is ever so necessary.

One of the better examples of Jesus and tough love is told in Matthew 12:46–50. Jesus was preaching to a crowd and one of his disciples told him that his mother and brothers were outside, asking to speak to him. Remember early in Jesus's ministry when he came to preach in his hometown of Nazareth? Some of the folks did not like what Jesus said and they wanted to stone him. Reportedly, his mother and family didn't try to protect him at that time. He escaped, but I always had a feeling that this caused a rift in the family. I wonder if his family came to his preaching either to mend fences or to take him home because they thought he had a demon. I surmise that Jesus wanted nothing to do with his family and rejected them with this pronouncement to his listeners: "Whoever does the will of my father in heaven is my brother and sister and mother." Implication: "Biologically, I am related, but I do not like you. Please go away." This was tough love in action. But somehow, by the end of Jesus's life, those broken fences were fixed because some members of his family carried on his mission after he was executed.

Agape demands tough love, which can be misinterpreted as not being unconditional. The parents who threw their drug-using child out of the house love that child so much that they were willing to risk alienating him to have him seek help. Giving a drug addict money and shelter and allowing him to be abusive does not help that person face reality. Tough love might.

INDIFFERENCE

Many people would say that the opposite of love is hate. I see the opposite of love as indifference. When someone hates me, I know it. I do not like being hated, but at least I know exactly where that person stands.

When someone is indifferent to me, I have a difficult time trying to figure out if that person is just having a bad day, dislikes me, is mad at me, or maybe was so involved in something else that he or she unintentionally ignored me. The only way to find out is to deal directly with the person and find out what the issue is.

As a therapist, I dealt with this issue frequently. In couples counseling, sometimes one partner was indifferent and it was difficult, even for me, to have that person answer my questions directly. I would get nebulous responses, such as "I don't know" or "That's interesting" or "I've never thought about that." But the person would never answer my questions. This passive-aggressive behavior can drive everyone crazy.

Watch out for folks who seem indifferent. They play games that can be deadly. Agape love allows other people to hate me or be indifferent, but I have found that indifference needs to be handled with tough love.

CONSCIENCE

I was raised with the idea "Let your conscience be your guide." Don't! As a disciple of agape, we have to look at how our conscience was formed.

Since I grew up in a Christian house, my conscience should have been pure. But we were white people living in a Black neighborhood. In my youth, I would sometimes engage in name-calling and fighting with the Black guys. I did some nasty things to them as they did to me. When I was twelve, some bigger Black boys stole my football right out of my hands in a public park and I could do nothing about it. Another time, they caught me on my roller skates going down a hill. They jumped out from behind a wall, tackled me, took off my skates, bashed me over the head with them, and ran away with them. Unfortunately, I carry a bit of that history in my brain, so my conscience can have negative feelings about Black people. Oh, I forgot to tell you about all the stuff I did to them, but back then I had a way of rationalizing my behavior. Therefore, I do not trust my conscience to be objective when dealing with some Black people. It has too much negative baggage. Agape is my foundation stone when dealing with Black people because unconditional love overrides any prejudices I might have.

I learned as a boy that Jews killed Jesus. I did not know any Jewish people, but as a result of ignorance I became antisemitic. I do not like it, but it is a reality, so I cannot let my conscience guide me—only agape.

When I was growing up, a gay person was a happy person. In about 1965, that word started referring to someone who was homosexual. As a young man, I had learned homosexuals were perverts and learned a slew of derogatory words about them. I did not know anyone who was gay, but my conscience told me gay people were bad. Agape changed my perspective. Unconditional love demands love for all. Today a person's sexual orientation makes no difference to agape or to me.

In my younger life, I was a racist, misogynist, homophobe, and sexist; I was critical of others who were not like me; and I was intolerant of people who were overweight or smoked or did not use correct English or voted the wrong way. My conscience might give me permission to act this way. But agape does not.

There is no question in my mind that my understanding about the LGBTQUI community has changed radically over the years because of agape and a desire to listen, grow, and evolve.

I can never let my conscience be my guide. Agape is my guiding principle.

JUSTICE

There is a great deal of difference between legal justice and moral justice. When I began writing this book (2020–2021), the United States was demonstrating many injustices (George Floyd was murdered by the police for being Black). I know there is not much justice for people who have dark skin, are poor, are homeless, have mental issues, or object to the bad behavior of too many police and law enforcement agencies. The injustice in our court system protects law enforcement personnel who do bad things. Our prisons and jails reek of great injustices, all under the heading "Department of Justice," which I see as anything but just.

My wife and I tutored inmates in jails and prisons for seven years. Too many times, we heard that all prisoners were bad. However, we found that a large majority of the people in prison were good people who allegedly had done something bad. Too many times, some of these "bad people" had not done anything bad. The cop who arrested them and presented false evidence was bad. Almost all our students were victims of poverty, abuse, drugs, mental issues, and a society that put a label on them that is impossible to lose. We loved our time tutoring these inmates but also saw the horrific dehumanization and cruelty that went on in the system.

Moral justice is founded on the principles of agape: giving unconditional love, granting lots of forgiveness, accepting people wherever they are on their life's journey, and genuinely caring about people as fellow human beings. I believe moral justice is love distributed.

Over and over again in the Gospels, Jesus practices moral justice. The lepers in Jesus's time were some of the outcasts of society. Unfortunately, lepers included not only those who had leprosy but also people who had any kind of skin issues. What people did to the lepers and those labeled as such was cruel and inhumane. But Jesus was not afraid to touch them, to deal with them, to heal them, or to show agape love to them, regardless of what society or the religious leaders thought.

I often refer to those in our society who are treated so unjustly as today's "lepers," and I believe the list is much longer now than in the time of Jesus. Just ask people of color, homeless people, poor people, those addicted to drugs, people with mental challenges, former prisoners, so many of those in the LGBTQUI community. They will tell you they are the victims of "justice," American style.

With the above reminders in mind, let us now look at some of the myriad of erroneous ideas that too many people consider the foundation stones of our faith. You might be taken aback about what Jesus's message isn't and even more surprised by what he talked about all the time. This is the Good News.

> *The opposite of love is not hate, it's indifference. The opposite of art is not ugliness, it's indifference. The opposite of faith is not heresy, it's indifference. And the opposite of life is not death, it's indifference.*
> —Elie Wiesel

CHAPTER 3

CONFUSERS

Treat others the same way you want to be treated.
—Luke 6:32

Consider this Daffy Definition: Beelzebug: Satan in the form of a mosquito that gets into your bedroom at three in the morning and can't be cast out.

Get ready for some daffy ideas.

I am not a big fan of the Golden Rule, especially as so many use it today: "He who has the gold, rules." In politics, our justice system, and social dynamics, this axiom seems to be the one that rules.

For me, agape rules, but other subjects are what I call "confusers."

My ideas about Jesus's message and who he was have changed radically since I started seminary. I now know a vastly different Jesus than I did sixty years ago.

At the start of courses I teach, I ask a series of questions to ascertain whether the class and I understand each other when we use certain words. For example, my first question always is, "Who or what is your idea of God?" I get a variety of answers, from "ruler of the universe" to "a figment of people's imagination."

When I ask people who they think Jesus is, again I receive a huge variety of responses, from "Son of God" to an imaginary figure.

My third question is, "What do you consider to be Jesus's primary message?" Here are a few of the answers.

The one I hear most often is "the Ten Commandments." My next question is, "Which version? There are three different choices in the Old Testament." I usually receive a blank stare. When I ask, "Do I have a volunteer to recite the Ten Commandments in order?" No one has ever spoken up.

The next most popular response is "the Golden Rule." I then might ask, "The positive version or the negative one?" That question usually goes unanswered.

My most frequent answer is "I don't know" or silence. People will often suggest that they have never really thought about the subject. They come to church because it feels good or they enjoy the sermons and the fellowship.

"The Beatitudes" is also a reply I occasionally hear. When I ask, "The first seven or all of them?" I hear silence. Sometimes I ask, "Do you like the version in Matthew or in Luke?" Most folks have no idea what I am asking.

My favorite answer, which, unfortunately, I seldom hear, is "the Great Commandment," also called the Summary of the Law. It is about agape.

Let us take a brief look at each of the above responses so that we can better understand why the Great Commandment is my favorite answer.

THE TEN COMMANDMENTS

The Ten Commandments are from the Old Testament, and as a Follower, I need to find my answers in the New Testament.

Early in my ministry, I was asked to do a preaching mission in Philadelphia at my father's church. It was just barely acceptable preaching because I was not mature enough as a Follower to be able to preach a strong gospel message.

How many versions of the Ten Commandments are there? The Old Testament has one version in Exodus 20:1–17 and another in Deuteronomy 5:6–21. A third version is found in Exodus 34:10–31, but it is not a complete set.

In Jewish religious history (not historical history), the commandments were given to Moses by God on Mount Sinai. The story says Moses went to the mountaintop to receive them. When he came back down, his people had behaved badly, so in anger, he smashed the tablets on the ground, which was not smart. He went back up the mountain and brought down a second copy.

It is well-established that other cultural groups have a similar set of guidelines. As a child, I had to memorize the Ten Commandments, but I could not recite them in order now. That is fine with me because they are simply a part of a religious history and have little or nothing to do with my faith. Agape is a summary of all these ten sayings.

Let's review each commandment.

1. *You shall have no other gods before me.* To which God are we referring? Is it the fundamentalist one? The Jewish one? The Muslim one? Or the one that you have imagined in your mind? I do not believe that God is an anthropomorphic being or that he/she/it rules earth or the universe. I see God as Creation.

2. *You shall make no idols.* Every religion seems to have its fair share of idols. My Episcopal church has many "idols": crosses, the Bible, *The Book of Common Prayer*, the bread and wine, the ecclesiastical vestments, the altar, and more. Over and over again, I see clergy and laity idolizing these material things. For me, they are just church stuff, often irrelevant and sometimes irreverent.

3. *You shall not take the name of the Lord your God in vain.* I promise I shall not say "goddammit" ever again, but this law is about more than cussing. It can mean respecting God, but my question is, Whose God? There are a whole bunch out there I shall never respect.

4. *You shall keep holy the Sabbath.* The Sabbath day starts Friday evening at sundown and extends until sundown on Saturday. My Saturdays are filled with "honey-dos" and projects. Most churchgoers set aside some part of Sunday to keep it "holy" but usually do whatever they feel like the rest of day. When I was a clergyperson, my Sundays were rather busy and not always holy. But I also believe every day of the week is holy and I need to live each one to the fullest.

5. *Honor your father and mother.* This commandment is a great idea—if your mother and father are worthy of honoring. As a psychotherapist and pastor, I have heard about some mothers and fathers who were not nice people, not worth honoring. I believe honor should not be automatic but is something that has to be earned. Some so-called parents need to be dishonored.

6. *You shall not murder.* This is a nice idea if you are not a police officer, a member of the military, a bodyguard, a security guard, or a prison guard. Probably the deadliest kinds of murder are gossiping, spreading conspiracy theories, rumor mongering, and bullying. All these behaviors kill people both literally and figuratively.

7. *You shall not commit adultery.* I have older friends who have lived with each other as husband and wife for years but are not married. Technically, they are committing adultery. The problem is that if they marry, they both would lose Social Security income. The label of *adultery* is also put on people who for one reason or another do not want to be legally married. They feel a legal document does not necessarily make a strong marriage and a legal divorce is always expensive, so why bother with a piece of paper? Are such folks violating this commandment? Yes, but they are doing what they think is best for them, and agape does not allow me to judge them.

8. *You shall not steal.* This is a good thought unless people are destitute and have no food. Do they steal food to keep their family alive or obey this commandment? How about people who are fighting wars and steal the enemies' supplies? Isn't that fair? Whether to label something as *stealing* can often depend on the circumstances surrounding the stealing.

9. *You shall not bear false witness against your neighbor.* Is this about gossip or dealing with someone with a different point of view? How many times have we heard about two people seeing the same accident but each having a most different interpretation of how that accident happened?
10. *You shall not covet.* I do not think coveting is the real issue. At some time in our lives, we all covet. The big problem comes when one acts on the coveted item.

I suspect it is obvious that the Ten Commandments do not do much to enhance my life. Let's move on.

THE GOLDEN RULE

The axiom of doing unto others as you would want them to do to you is not helpful to me. It is too simplistic and one of those sayings that sounds good but is not very realistic. I could never apply the Golden Rule and play competitive sports, be an officer in the Marine Corps sending my troops into action, a police officer, a schoolteacher or administrator, or an effective parent. My parents did not use this rule while raising me, and there is no way we would have ever used this rule in raising our daughters. Watching them parent their own children, I can see that they, too, have raised their children using tough love, not the Golden Rule.

"I DON'T KNOW!"

Too many people who go to church have little or no idea what Jesus's main message was. Why is this? My honest answer is based on the fact that most clergy feel forced to preach to the "comfortable pew"—not rocking the boat if they want an ongoing salary. Too many churchgoers do not want to be challenged by the pastor's remarks on a Sunday morning. They much prefer "sweetness and light" and leaving the church feeling comfortable.

I also think that too many institutional churches and their clergy do not want their people to think. They would much rather tell people what to think than give them information and allow them to work out the answers for themselves. The church, like so many other institutions, wants to control, and one of the best ways to do that is to tell the members how to think, vote, and lead their daily lives.

"I don't know" can also be a way of getting off the hook for a series of reasons:

- The person has an answer but is not sure it is the response the asker wants to hear.
- The person has never thought about this issue.
- The person has a stock answer comes to mind—"Jesus died for my sins" or "Jesus is God or His Son"—but feel safer saying, "I don't know."

- The person has an answer but fears people might think it is stupid, so he or she says, "I don't know."

I believe "I don't know" is a sad commentary. It says to me that the clergy are not teaching or even preaching about agape, often a controversial subject when dealing with the LGBTQUI community or women's rights. It also says that too many churches are not sure why they exist but do so for all sorts of devious reasons having little or nothing to do with Jesus.

THE BEATITUDES

Sometimes the Beatitudes are referred to as the Sermon on the Mount. The short edition is found in the Gospel of Matthew 5:3–12. Some scholars believe that the Beatitudes continue through Matthew 7:29 because this whole segment deals with utopian behavior in the first century CE. Most scholars agree that although all these sayings were attributed to Jesus, they are really ideas that Matthew plagiarized from Judaism as well as other cultures and placed in one section of his gospel, making Jesus responsible.

Dictionary.com defines *beatitude* as "extreme blessedness: exalted happiness." One can find sayings similar to the Beatitudes in the Old Testament, the apocryphal writings, and other parts of the New Testament.

In some of the later translations of the Beatitudes, the translators have reinterpreted the word *blessed* to mean "congratulations." For example, the Beatitude "Blessed are the poor" becomes "Congratulations to the poor." If I were poor, I would not be comforted by being blessed and would be offended at being congratulated. The poor need money and opportunities, not a Kingdom or imaginary heaven.

Some envision the Beatitudes as more of an eschatological (having to do with death and last things) statement rather than a first-century Jewish ethical law. Bottom line: the Beatitudes are not at all helpful to me as I lead my life today, and I see them more as Matthew's wish list than Jesus's words.

THE GREAT COMMANDMENT

For me, the Great Commandment is the heart of Jesus's message, the foundation stone of the Christian religion, and the guiding light for the institutional church. It took me some fifteen years to evolve to this position.

My biggest disappointment is that I do not hear enough church folks shouting it from the rooftops.

Sometime in his life, Jesus had learned that Deuteronomy 6:5—"You shall love the Lord your God with all your heart, and with all your soul, and with all your might"—was an extremely powerful statement. He combined it with Leviticus 19:18, "You shall love your neighbor as yourself." Then Jesus claimed, "Everything in the law and the prophets hang on these two commandments" (Matt. 22:40).

The Gospel of Mark (12:31) says it a little differently: "There is no other commandment greater than these."

I see this as the summation of all that Jesus preached and taught. I hear him saying that this commandment to love is more powerful than the 613 laws the Jewish people followed and even more powerful than all the Old Testament prophets' sayings.

These words are the difference between the Old Testament and the New Testament as well as the primary difference between Judaism and Christianity. Luke (10:28) ends this section with "do this and you shall live." The Great Commandment, all about love, is the elixir of life.

Let us now examine some of the many problems folks face when they interpret the resurrection/Easter stories literally. The resurrection is not what you have been told for years, and you might be taken aback when you hear that it is not even true in a literal sense.

I don't care how much Scripture you quote. How do you treat people?
—Unknown

CHAPTER 4

THE PROBLEMS WITH A DEAD MAN WALKING

So they went out and fled from the tomb, for terror and amazement had seized them; and they said nothing more to anyone, for they were afraid.
—Mark 16:8

A man, his wife, and his rather cranky father-in-law took a trip to the Holy Lands. Shortly after they arrived, the father-in-law had a severe heart attack and died.

The undertaker said, "We have two choices. We can bury him here in this holy place for $300, where he will spend eternity, or we can send him back to California for $10,000."

Without hardly a moment's hesitation, the man said, "We'll send him back to California."

The undertaker was taken aback and asked why. If his father-in-law were buried there, the man would save a great deal of money and it would be a lovely place to come and visit.

The man then asked, "Didn't you have a man here two thousand years ago who died and then came back to life?"

The undertaker said, "Yes, but that was Jesus a long time ago. It hasn't happened since."

The man replied, "Yes, but I can't take the chance."

I can't take a chance that you don't have the following information because it is paramount to understanding my major premise.

For all sorts of reasons, gentiles insist on reading the Bible's dead-man-walking stories as the literal truth. They were never written as history, and it is important to understand that they are metaphors. Once that distinction is made, we can learn why they are metaphors and how to interpret them.

I believe in the power of the resurrection—as a metaphor. It took me at least forty years to arrive at this stage of my thinking. First I had to go to seminary to eradicate my Sunday school theology. Then a fire engine broadsiding me on my motorcycle and killing my friend Brad convinced me that there is NoOneUpThere. The accident happened because of free will. Within a few years, I had substituted the word *Creation* for the word *God*, and then the road was clear for me to look at the historical Jesus versus the fictitious one. I liked what I saw and found that the historical Jesus appealed much more in my quest for a workable christ.

That christ has become my Christ. With that in mind, let's discuss some ideas about the resurrection stories.

TIMING

The first time anyone read a resurrection story was more than fifty years after Jesus died, in the Gospel of Matthew.

Mark, written mostly about 70 CE, also has a resurrection story in 16:9–21. However, these verses were added at least a hundred years later. The original story ends at 16:8 with some of the disciples running away from the tomb.

Why might additional stories suddenly appear? Let us start with the fact that Jesus had two major strikes against his being recognized as the Messiah.

Strike 1. According to Celsus (second-century Greek philosopher and anti-Christian), Mary, Jesus's mother, was raped by a Roman soldier named Tiberius Julius Abdes Pantera (22 BCE–40 CE), thus labeling Jesus "illegitimate," perhaps unfit for Messiahship. Making God responsible for the birth of Jesus adds great credibility to Jesus, the long-awaited Messiah. (Do I believe the story about Tiberius? Probably not, but it is more reasonable than NoOneUpThere having sex with Mary.)

Strike 2. Jesus was a criminal, a felon, crucified for the serious crime of sedition (treason) or inciting people to rebel against the Roman authority by claiming to be king, which he never did. Being a felon is not a positive trait for the *Christ* (the Greek word for Messiah). But, when the crucifixion and resurrection of Jesus are designed as God's plan, it expunges his record of sedition.

Both negatives were easily fixed with a "divine plan."

Here is a reality that must be faced. No records—not a birth or death certificate, eyewitnesses, or even a journal—substantiate the accounts of Jesus's birth and death. Nativity and resurrection stories are fabrications. But in doing midrash (Jewish biblical interpretation) on all such stories, we find some great truths. For example, the Nativity stories show us that Jesus's beginning was humble, he came from poverty, daily life was hard, and Jesus is one of us.

LACK OF CONSENSUS

Some twenty-three different accounts were written in the first two centuries CE about the life of Jesus, his messages, and his close Followers. Only Matthew, Luke and Acts, John, and Peter share a resurrection story. Peter's gospel is simply a composite of Matthew, Luke and Acts, and John. Mark's resurrection story was an addition a hundred or more years after the gospel was originally written.

It is a well-established fact that John never intended to write a biography about Jesus. His is a gospel full of allegories and metaphors told through imaginary stories but containing great truths. John is all about agape.

So only 10 percent of all the writings about Jesus contain a resurrection story and each of them is different from the others. For instance, John places Jesus's mother at the foot of the cross. By that time, Mother Mary would have been in her fifties when the average life span for a woman was thirty-five. She lived in Nazareth, so Jerusalem was about a ten- to fourteen-day blazing-hot uphill walk away. That is not an easy task. I think John's school fabricated that story, especially since Roman soldiers at a crucifixion would have never allowed friends or family to be anywhere close to the criminal.

TWENTY-FIRST CENTURY

Today we have so much more information about everything than people did two thousand years ago. However, many Christians consider science, technology, biblical scholarship, astronomy, archaeology, and biology to be shams and enemies of the church. They feel they or their church might fall apart if anything were to change, which could force people to think differently. And as many of us know, religion is not friendly to change.

Don't forget the bumper sticker that reads, "Religion is for people who don't like to think." There is a degree of truth in it.

I have found that new discoveries in most fields are very helpful not only in my theological growth but also in my daily living. Seeing the resurrection stories as metaphors has been especially powerful. A hundred years ago, the church would not have allowed me to doubt, question, or dispel so much of its dogma and doctrine without being tried for heresy. Today I can and must challenge ancient ideas. (The church still does not like it.) However, that is how we grow.

The most important factor that keeps me open to change is this: regardless of the changing world, Jesus's message of agape is as relevant today as it was in the early history of Judaism (Deuteronomy and Leviticus) or Jesus's time. This same message will be true as long as people exist.

DEATH

I know that four minutes after I die, my body starts to decompose. This process never stops until I am "dust and to dust you shall return" (Genesis 3:19). I could never believe that Jesus undeaded and came back looking like a Scandinavian with well-coiffed hair and manicured nails, wearing a flowing white nightgown and standing about six inches off the ground. But I can and do believe in the daily presence of a first-century Palestinian Jew whose message of agape has changed me and many others in the last two thousand years. Jesus and his message are alive, well, and living among us.

A dead man walking is a fairy tale that makes no sense in the twenty-first century, but as a metaphor about how to change life's darkest experiences into light, it is transformative.

SITZ IM LEBEN

Sitz im Leben is a German phrase meaning "situation in life." It is a process whereby one studies a situation in light of what might have happened in real life. I want to describe the process of crucifixion in the Roman Empire in the first century CE, especially in the Roman-occupied area of Jerusalem. This is not specifically about Jesus's crucifixion but about what happened at most crucifixions in those days. Remember, there were no eyewitnesses when Jesus and Pilate were talking or when Jesus was with the Roman soldiers, and no one was close to Jesus when he was crucified.

We have read the stories about Jesus's crucifixion in the gospels, but these tales were produced some fifty to seventy years after Jesus had been executed. It would have been almost impossible for any live witnesses to still have been around at that time.

No one knows precisely how the Romans crucified Jesus. Was he nailed to the posts or tied? Did he have a footrest or did he just hang? Did he really refuse the wine and myrrh sedative? How many others were crucified with him? Why do we have three gospels that differ in details? The answer to all the above questions: we don't have any idea and never shall.

We cannot forget that Jesus was crucified as a criminal, charged with sedition—as a pretender king inciting rebellion against the Roman Empire. Once convicted, the prisoner immediately went to prison. There was no such thing as bail for that crime. We have no idea if the Roman soldiers actually brutalized Jesus, but we do know that brutalizing prisoners was very common. We also know that the Roman soldiers disliked Jews because the Jews caused so many problems, like stealing supplies, rebelling, and even killing soldiers. An important objective of the Roman soldiers was to dehumanize prisoners who were slated to be crucified. Beating prisoners, mocking them, jamming a crown of thorns onto a prisoner's head, stripping a person naked, and publicly humiliating someone was a good start. (Unfortunately, this sounds like some prison guards today.)

Roman soldiers guarded the crucifixion site. Once a criminal appeared to have died, a centurion, an experienced noncommissioned officer overseeing a hundred soldiers, would validate the death of the victim. Just a little aside: if the centurion did not do his job thoroughly in pronouncing the prisoner dead, the centurion could be crucified the next day. This little fact eradicates conspiracy theories such as Jesus merely swooned, someone took Jesus's place, or the guards were bribed to let Jesus escape.

Then one of two things would happen. Some dead prisoners were left on the cross for the wild animals to munch on that night. The more problematic criminals were taken to the city dump, called Gehenna, thrown in the burning trash, and totally consumed by the fire. The Romans were extremely careful not to allow one iota of the corpse to remain intact for fear that someone would take a morsel of the criminal and use it as a trophy of martyrdom or worship.

Why is this sadistic portrayal so important? Artists have painted pictures or sculpted statues of Jesus surrounded by Mother Mary (by now old), Mary of Magdala (maybe Jesus's wife?), Joseph of Arimathea (an imaginary figure), and others at the foot of the cross. Dead Jesus lying in the lap of his mother is pastoral, but *Sitz im Leben* says that would have never happened, especially to a political criminal such as Jesus. No civilians were allowed near the criminals.

Sitz im Leben also says no body would have been left for anyone to bury. The Romans would have never allowed it. And without a body, there could be no such thing as a physical resurrection.

These stories are fictitious, maybe based on similar stories from past history or mythology. In my book *Cramming for the Finals: New Ways of Looking at Old Church Ideas*, I list nine look-alike crucifixion or resurrection stories that appeared in other cultures in the past.

Kersey Graves wrote a book on this topic, *The World's Sixteen Crucified Saviors*, if you would like further information.

SIGMUND FREUD

How does one go from a gory description of crucifixion to Freud, the famous nineteenth-century psychiatrist, psychoanalyst, author, Jewish atheist, and agitator? It's related to his fascination with religion. He described religion as infantile and foreign to reality. At first, I was bothered by that description, especially as a clergyperson. But the more I thought about it, the more it made sense. Not much in the Bible is historical history. The writings are religious history, which cares more about the underlying truths than facts.

Religion can be and, for the most part, is infantile, at least from my vantage point as a Follower, Episcopalian, pastor, and active church participant. In our prayers, creeds, and discussions, we refer to God as a "Father," sort of humanlike but perfect. (There is no such thing as perfect except in the eyes of the beholder.) He is everywhere, all the time, running everything. He is an authoritative figure, and we are naughty children who need to repent so maybe He will rescue us—like by having his son murdered. God, the Father, never lets us grow up. Having someone die for our sins never forces us to be responsible for our mess-ups. A Savior keeps rescuing us rather than teaching us to work through our issues. A Heavenly Father, an Almighty God, Eternal God, O Lord our Governor, and all the other titles we give NoOneUpThere as we pray and to whom we give our daily, weekly, and monthly lists of what She or He is to do for us (heal, comfort, fix, change, etc.) often can be used as an excuse for us to do nothing. It is Her or His problem.

I see my religion as a religion for grownups who need to be the hands and feet that make agape happen.

SPACE EXPLORATION

With the advent of new technology and the space age, including the Hubble Space Telescope, all the church's ancient dogma, doctrine, and tradition were challenged. Once valid information about the universe became public knowledge, most of the so-called foundation stones of the institutional church became obsolete. For instance, we know that when Jesus was declared dead by the centurion, within four minutes his body started decaying, and that process moved quickly in the hot climate of the Holy Lands.

The idea of Jesus ascending to wherever makes no sense. For one, his body would have been rather decayed (and stinky) fifty days after he died, when he supposedly ascended. If he *had* ascended (it would take some extremely powerful rockets and special space suits to go through the atmosphere), he would still be in orbit.

Do we really wonder why so many people have no interest in becoming involved in institutional religion? We do not deal with reality. The bottom line: all the reality in the universe is not going to destroy the power of agape, as shared by Jesus.

MIDRASH

I defined *midrash* in the beginning of this book. It means "biblical interpretation" and it is what Jewish biblical scholars do when they interpret stories in the Old Testament. They all know that each story as written is not necessarily real. But inside that story is a great deal of truth.

The story of Adam and Eve is not real and was never written to explain how humanity developed. It is about the problem of free will. At first, Adam and Eve did not have any—they were totally obedient. But then they made a choice (free will), and many suggest that their choice was not a good one (eating the forbidden fruit), so they (and we) had to pay a price for the rest of their (and our) lives. The story of Adam and Eve appears over and over on the six o'clock news every night, as free will often makes unfortunate choices. Humanity keeps making the same mistakes over and over.

The three resurrection stories are not about a dead man walking, which taken literally is totally ridiculous. But if we do midrash to the story, then these resurrection stories can become an unbelievably transforming experience in one's life.

I am not sure where Annie's and my life would be if we had not used this metaphor with the birth of our multichallenged second child. Most of the folks we know who have a child with challenges are divorced. Such an event puts a real strain on a marriage. Too many of these children then end up in single-parent families, which makes raising such children even more difficult on parents, siblings, relatives, and friends. If one does not have a solid theology, often God is blamed and people either hate God, who "planned" this, or worship God, who "sent" such a child because they were rotten sinners.

Using the resurrection stories as metaphors, Annie and I took our Good/Bad Friday (suddenly becoming parents of a child we never imagined we would have) and, using all the tools of agape, turned it into an Easter where we opened new doors into our own lives, our children's lives, and the lives of so many of our family and friends.

Looking back, we made a silk purse out of a sow's ear thanks to resurrection theology.

Now let us look more closely at the resurrection stories as metaphors. Make certain you are seated for the next chapter because this might be the kicker that changes the course of the institutional church, hopefully, the course of civilization, and better yet, your life. It is the elixir, and it's radical.

The church has taught us that Jesus died for our sins, is the Son of God and we're all born bad. The church has been marketing it for centuries but consider the reality about this. For so many reasons, it does not make sense. Examining it truthfully enables us to look at another alternative that does make sense.

> *Jesus was a Middle Eastern bleeding heart liberal socialist who challenged authority and had convictions—everything conservatives dislike about Progressive Christians.*
> —Unknown

CHAPTER 5

THE POWER OF THE RESURRECTION— AS A METAPHOR

You shall love the Lord your God with all your heart, with all your
soul and with all your mind. This is the first and great commandment.
And the second is like it: you shall love your neighbor as yourself.
On these two commandments hang all the law and the prophets.
—Mark 12:30–31

A lawyer, a priest, and a politician died and were waiting at the Pearly Gates when Saint Peter came out, welcomed them, and said that he needed to give each of them a little test before they could enter. He called the lawyer first and asked if he minded taking a test and the lawyer said no. So Peter said, "Spell God." The lawyer replied, "G-O-D." Peter then said, "Perfect! Please enter and enjoy eternity." The priest was next and the same thing happened. Peter called the politician, and when he asked if he minded if he gave him a little test, the politician yelled, "My whole life I have been tested by voters, pundits, and other politicians. They call me awful names, make up lies, and attack my family. I hate tests, but if you must, go ahead."

Peter said, "Spell Tchaikovsky."

(Disclaimer: I don't believe in heaven, hell, judgment, or Pearly Gates, but I sure like jokes about them.)

I can never spell Tchaikovsky. Can you? Now we won't get into heaven, but that's okay. It doesn't exist, like so many different concepts about life after death.

Paul's story about Jesus dying for our sins has been tattooed onto our belief system, but we need to make the distinction between stories told as metaphors and stories told as history. Using resurrection as a metaphor, we can see by example how the metaphor works in real life and that the good Samaritan and prodigal son parables are stories about agape, which is a segue into how so much of the New Testament is about agape.

First, let us look at a couple of definitions from Dictionary.com:

metaphor: "A figure of speech in which a term or phrase is applied to something to which it is not literally applicable in order to suggest a resemblance."

resurrection: "The act of rising from the dead."

The opening joke is about a place that doesn't exist and a test that will never happen—exactly like a literal resurrection, which is impossible.

For me, the resurrection is a powerful figure of speech having nothing to do with Jesus actually arising from the dead. Instead, it is a metaphor about changing a figurative death into life, a negative into a positive—a transformation. It took me years of questioning, listening to new ideas, and rethinking to arrive at this conclusion.

SEEING THE GOSPELS FROM A NEW PERSPECTIVE

In seminary, the summer I helped a professor find Old Testament quotations in the New Testament (which would later become the subject of my doctoral thesis), I discovered how closely the life of Jesus parallels Old Testament predictions and prophecies. I started to realize that maybe the Jesus in the gospels was designed around those predictions and prophecies. The New Testament contains no history about Christianity because there was no such word or religion until the second century CE. The Jesus movement started within Judaism.

Around 88 CE, the Followers of Jesus were expelled from Judaism because they believed that Jesus was the Messiah. Orthodox Jews had no interest in a poor, uneducated Jewish peasant as their Messiah (in Greek, *Christ*). At this stage, we start to see the exodus of Jewish people and the diminishing of their new religion. They are replaced by gentiles and the influence of Hellenism. But the foundation stones of this now new religion, later to be called Christianity are almost entirely Jewish. I did not leave seminary fully understanding this. The final reality was brought home in Bishop John S. Spong's book *Liberating the Gospels: Reading the Bible with Jewish Eyes*, published in 1996.

Looking at the gospels through Jewish eyes was not easy for me. I am not Jewish and do not have those eyes, which start to develop at birth and are nurtured through living the life of a Jew. I do not know Hebrew nor the subtleties of the Jewish culture and religion. I have never had to face the reality of antisemitism, which never seems to go away.

However, I did understand that when Jews tell the stories of their heritage, most of the time the stories themselves are not true, but they contain great truths. It is my job to tease out those truths (with the help of rabbis and biblical scholars) and to share them. I also learned that one might read the same stories numerous times and find different truths. In the Jewish process of midrash, no one has the absolute truth and all findings are valid. There is no absolute right or wrong. This makes sense to me but not to many Christians; almost every denomination says, "Believe what we say or leave."

My church is not going to allow me to be a priest and also proclaim that I am an A-theist or that Jesus was not God nor his Son but simply a fellow human. However, I know I confuse people when I state, "But Jesus is still my Christ." Some will say, "To be a Christian, one has to believe that Jesus was the Son of God and died for our sins." My only retort: "Who says? I think a Christian is someone who believes that Jesus of Nazareth is his or her Christ."

We know that the resurrection stories never appeared in written form until more than fifty years after Jesus died. Paul (always a Jew)—the first known writer for this new offshoot of Judaism—in letters written ten to fifteen years after the Jewish Jesus had been executed, used the word *resurrection* but with a different meaning (explained below).

We also know that no one would have been allowed to take notes when Jesus and Pilate were talking or when Jesus was on the cross, so accounts of those conversations were fictitious. Nor would anyone (even the fictitious Joseph of Arimathea) have been allowed to take Jesus's body for burial.

Each of the three stories about that fictitious first Easter is different. The writers had different resources and biases, but the metaphor is the same: with the tools Jesus gives us, we can change a negative into a positive and we can experience a transformation.

Perhaps there was also another reason for telling a resurrection story. Jesus was crucified because of criminal charges. Those charges would be expunged if God had designed this experience as part of a divine plan.

Unfortunately, in the twenty-first century, this plan makes God a child abuser because he planned and oversaw the horrendous death of his son.

I want to share a rather obvious observation about life: all human beings have negative events in their lives, sometimes even on a daily basis. Some are huge—for example, three members of your family came down with COVID-19. Two died and one spent two months in a hospital. That person has been released from the hospital but is having long-lasting health issues. That is huge!

Or today's tragedy could be about a stubbed toe, inconvenient but not hard to live with. Both incidents remind us of the following:

- Negative stuff happens to everyone throughout our lives.
- The negatives are not the work of some god making bad things happen to good people. Free will is still alive and well.
- Some folks know how to move through the negatives, other folks do not have the skills or become stuck on the negatives.
- Forgiveness of self or others is often the biggest obstacle.
- Some people do not want any help with the challenges. Maybe they feel embarrassed, think that getting help is a sign of weakness (for me, it's a sign of strength), refuse to recognize the problem, or try to solve it by taking the easy way out.
- Other folks want to solve negative issues quickly and will accept help so they can move forward.
- Jesus gives us a tool—a tool I consider the elixir of life—called agape, unconditional love, with lots of forgiveness, acceptance, and caring. This tool is guaranteed to turn our Good/Bad Fridays into Easters. It is transformative and takes a great deal of pain out of daily living.

MY PERSONAL EASTER STORY

Here is an example of one of my many resurrection life experiences. Our middle daughter was born on Maui in 1965. She was conceived in France, where we were living at the time, and Anne had had a difficult pregnancy. Our daughter was born a month overdue, weighed only five pounds, looked as if she had been "overcooked," with red dots all over her body, had a mature cataract in her right eye, was severely to profoundly deaf, had a heart murmur, had a nystagmus (involuntary eye movement) in both eyes, was epileptic, and had mild cerebral palsy. The day this child was born was an extremely difficult Good/Bad Friday for us and our daughter, and her condition would keep throwing new Good/Bad Fridays our way. It still does.

Being faith-based people, we knew God had nothing to do with it. Our daughter was conceived because of free will, as we made the decision to continue growing our family.

We met people from the March of Dimes organization, who recommended that we place our eighteen-month-old daughter into a hospital in Honolulu for a thorough six-week evaluation. We did. The final recommendation: leave Maui as soon as possible and move to Honolulu to take advantage of the excellent resources there for our deaf and legally blind daughter. This diagnosis, which had been a Good/Bad Friday, became an Easter.

Now I had to face another Good/Bad Friday. I would have to resign from my duties at my church on Maui where I had distinguished myself in many different areas. This was painful and detrimental to my upward career path in the ministry, but I knew we could make this another Easter.

Throughout this entire venture, our faith played a major role. The doctor in charge of the March of Dimes was an Episcopalian, and I know she gave us special attention. Our daughter was placed in a program with two teachers and four students. She progressed rapidly as she learned how to live as a deaf and legally blind person. Each of these events was called an Easter.

I experienced another Easter when a large parish rehired me to revive a dying youth program. When I left this church and its youth group to go to France in 1963, the program had 350 teenagers involved. Four years later, the number had dwindled to forty and the rector gave me carte blanche to develop innovative ways to attract young people to the church.

Unfortunately, too many couples with a differently abled child divorce. The pressure is horrendous. Annie and I did not try to blame anyone or anything because that would have been a waste of time. Our marriage became stronger because we became heavily involved as a team in the deaf, the blind, and the deaf-and-blind communities, another hugely transforming experience.

We have had so many new, rich experiences because of this daughter.

I have ministered in prisons, and Anne and I tutored in jails for years. We have seen our students go from school dropouts, drug addicts, and victims who were unsuccessful in whatever they did to college graduates with successful adult lives. Unconditional love is always transforming.

I worked with gangs, went to court with gang members, helped them obtain their high school degree, taught them how to apply and interview for jobs, protected them from the police, and gave them all the agape I had. Many of them became productive members of their communities rather than gangsters. This is what Easter is for me and many of them.

Caring for and about "the least" (Matt. 25:40) is one of the most important aspects of agape. This is how one makes *Jesus* an action verb, not a noun. Creation is action.

OTHER EASTERS IN THE BIBLE

Let us now return to two stories (introduced in chapter 1) that exemplify the power of the Easter truths.

First is "Agape Dad" ("The Prodigal Son," Luke 15:11–32), and second, "Agape in Action" ("The Good Samaritan," Luke 10:25–37).

In "Agape Dad," both the younger son and his father were having their Good/Bad Fridays. The son had disgraced the family name and himself. He was desperate. The father knew he had lost a son, maybe both literally and figuratively. Son and Dad were in lots of pain. The son buried his pride and returned home. The father buried his disappointment and anger and unconditionally accepted his son back. The father forgave him and welcomed him as he was (no lectures or punishment), and they both were transformed with a new beginning.

However, the elder son did not bury his anger. It controlled him, and his Good/Bad Friday stayed that way (his choice). His anger ruled his life. Sound familiar?

As a psychotherapist, I spent a great deal of time working with people like the elder brother, who refused to forgive and move on. Many times, anger kills (figuratively and sometimes literally) the person who refuses to forgive.

Now let us look at "Agape in Action" again. The severely beaten Jewish man was almost dead. The Samaritan could have passed by with, "Oh, he's a Galilean Jew. Let him die." But, no, the Samaritan stopped and saved the man's life by giving him agape.

I wonder if the Samaritan also had an Easter. In my congregations, I have been involved in a program called "Stephen Ministry," where we trained (for fifty hours) laity to learn the art of listening—a great healing gift. Once people were trained, we assigned each to a person going through some sort of life crisis. The two would meet weekly for about an hour. The person going through the crisis certainly appreciated the Stephen Minister, but over and over I heard the Stephen Minister expressing an Easter feeling—his or her life had also been transformed.

Jesus put it this way: "Those who want to save their life will lose it, and those who lose their life [doing agape] for my sake will save it" (Luke 9:24).

The fun thing about being progressive is that one is allowed to look at many different ideas because all are acceptable. This is what I believe today, but that could change tomorrow because that is how I grow, evolve, and transform. The ideas about agape are not new. They have been around for centuries, but some in the church suppressed them. Fortunately, for a progressive, beliefs can always be in a state of flux, except for the Great Commandment, which has been around for over three thousand years. That is the constant that can never go out of date.

Love makes the world go 'round, so let us look at some of the many passages in the New Testament that remind us of the power of agape.

Before religion made it all about what we believe, Jesus was about how we love.
—Unknown

CHAPTER 6

IT'S ABOUT LOVE

For all the law is fulfilled in a single commandment:
you shall love your neighbor as yourself.
—Galatians 5:14

A duck waddled into a grocery store and quacked, "Any strawberries?" The clerk replied, "Dumb duck, get out of here." A little while later, the duck appeared again. "Any strawberries?" The angry clerk yelled, "Beat it!" The duck was persistent and came back again with the same question. The clerk threatened, "If you don't get out of here and stay out, I'm going to nail your feet to the floor." He chased the duck out. But the smart duck returned later and asked, "Any nails?" The furious clerk said, "Of course not, we're a grocery store." Immediately, the duck replied, "Any strawberries?"

In Jesus's time and in the early church, the power of agape was always there, but in the twenty-first century, more and more church people and leaders are seeing agape as the most important message of Jesus, and for them the idea of God ordering his son to be executed in the most horrendous fashion for our mess-ups, which never cease happening, is not resonating. The idea of unconditional love is starting to take a strong foothold. Many young people endorse it but are leery of the church.

I feel a little like the duck, very repetitious. I keep wanting the church to believe that Jesus, his ministry, and his message were about love, not a dead man walking, but I am fighting two thousand years of Jesus dying for our sins.

Let us look in the New Testament and see if the writers might agree with the premise that the gospel is about agape, forgiveness, and the resurrection metaphor.

PAUL

Since Paul was the first, as far as we know, to write about Jesus and his messages, let us start with him. Remember these facts:

1. Paul was born, lived, and died a Jew. He was a highly educated religious leader in Judaism.

2. He never met, heard, or saw the man Jesus, so everything he says about Jesus is either hearsay or fabricated.

3. The authentic letters of Paul are 1 Thessalonians, Galatians, 1 and 2 Corinthians, Philippians, Philemon, and Romans. The other letters attributed to Paul—Ephesians, Colossians, 2 Thessalonians, 1 and 2 Timothy, and Titus—were not written by Paul, but we know little about the authors and their agenda.

4. Most of Paul's letters were not written as theological textbooks but were personal letters he sent to churches he had started or was going to start. Many of them contain commentary on practical and ethical matters, as well as his understanding of the role of Jesus in the Jewish/gentile congregations he had started throughout the Diaspora (see #5 below). The exception would be his letter to the Romans, which is very doctrinal but based on Judaism.

5. Paul traveled extensively throughout the northwest Middle East and eastern Europe (today, Lebanon, Syria, Turkey, and Greece), ministering in synagogues and talking about Jesus to his fellow Jews and interested gentiles.

6. There was no such word as *Christian* in Paul's lifetime. That word was first recorded around 90 CE.

7. Paul became a Follower of the Anointed (a Jewish denomination) some three years after Jesus was crucified, about the year 36–39 CE, and was executed in Rome, under Emperor Nero, about 64 CE.

8. Paul is *not* my Christ. He is simply a historical figure in the early years of what would later (about 88 CE) become Christianity. Jesus is my Christ, and I take my marching orders from him.

I contend that Paul fabricated a Jesus who suited his theology. His Jesus did not resemble the historical one nor the one found in the gospels and Acts (which were not written in Paul's lifetime). Paul felt Jesus was the long-awaited Messiah who died for our sins and was trying to convince his fellow Jews that the Messiah had come.

Here's how Jesus became Paul's sacrificial lamb who died for our sins.

First, Yom Kippur was a time in the Jewish liturgical year when the high priest at the Temple in Jerusalem would take two unblemished goats to use as "scapegoats" for the sins of the Jews. On one goat, the sins were ceremoniously attached and then the goat was set free in the wilderness, carrying all the sins of the Jews away. The second goat was offered as a purification sacrifice on the altar in the holy of holies. Once that goat had been sacrificed, the Jewish people were cleansed until the next Yom Kippur.

In his letters, Paul replaced sacrificing the goat on the altar with Jesus's crucifixion and birthed the idea that Jesus died for our sins. I do not believe this and have no interest in a God who would sacrifice his son for my mess-ups. That is immoral, illegal today, and irresponsible.

Paul's concept of Christianity has been around for some two thousand years, but in my lifetime, I have not noticed that sin has diminished an iota. In my thinking, Paul's sacrificial Jesus was a waste of a nice Jewish man as well as a silly idea.

Second, when Paul used the word *resurrection*, it did not have the same meaning as it does in the church today. Paul's resurrected Jesus then became God, who had conquered death. It was figurative, not literal. In 1 Corinthians 15:35–50, Paul says that a resurrected Jesus is spiritual and incorporeal (not of matter). But lest we forget, Paul's God was the one who lived above the third tier of the flat earth in His many mansions. Paul's earth was the center of the universe, and the sun revolved around it. He had no idea that the universe contains some two to four trillion galaxies and that a human on his or her own cannot survive more than three miles above the earth's surface.

Was Paul aware of Jesus's message about the power of agape? We do know that none of the gospels had been written before Paul died. Perhaps he had become familiar with Jesus through the circulation of the oral stories about this charismatic preacher and teacher.

Paul's first letter to the church in Corinth, the thirteenth chapter, called "the love letter," says, "Faith, hope, love abide; but the greatest of these is love" (1 Cor. 13:13). Some scholars have questioned whether this passage originated with Paul, but regardless, it is probably one of the most often quoted passages from the Bible because it is all about agape.

It does appear that Paul was familiar with the Great Commandment, about loving self, neighbor, and God (see Rom. 8:28, 12:10, and 13:8–10; Gal. 5:14; and 1 Thes. 4:9).

Here are a couple of other quotations from Paul's letters that reinforce agape. In Romans 13:10, Paul says, "Love is the fulfilling of the law." In Romans 13:9, Paul lists some of the commandments and then says that they, "and any other commandments, are summed up in this word: 'You shall love your neighbor as yourself.'" In these two quotes, Paul says that if one practices agape, one does not need any laws. This is a utopian idea, but it is also my contention that with agape, we do not need laws or theology. The church will probably not agree. It seems to like rules and laws.

AGAPE BIBLICAL QUOTES FROM OTHER WRITERS

Now we will look at a few of my favorite biblical quotes that show agape.

Judging

Judging is a difficult word. Matthew 7:1 says, "Do not judge." But all day long, we make judgments, whether we are driving a vehicle, talking politics, seeing a person who is different, or listening to someone expressing an opinion, to name a few. If I am truly living unconditional love, there is no room for judgment because I must accept all people, no matter where they are on their life's journey. I do know, however, that I need a guideline, one of which I find in Matthew 7:5: "First take the log out of your own eye, and then you will see clearly to take the speck out of your neighbor's eye."

One story tells about some religious leaders who were testing Jesus—again. They thought they had Jesus trapped, and no matter what he said, Jesus would be wrong. The story tells about a woman who allegedly had committed adultery. They wanted to know what Jesus would do with this woman, knowing that his answer could result in her being stoned to death and maybe a trial for him. Jesus stooped down and started doodling on the ground. Then, without even looking up, he stated, "Let anyone among you who is without sin be the first to throw a stone at her" (John 8:7). The religious leaders quietly crept away, without throwing a stone. We who live agape can never throw a stone; unconditional love stops that.

Forgiving

One of the key components of agape is forgiveness, which needs to be offered easily and quickly.

In Matthew 18:21–22, Peter asked Jesus a question: "'How often should I forgive? As many as seven times?' Jesus said to him, 'Not seven times, but I tell you seventy-seven times.'" *Seventy-seven* is a code word for an infinite number of times. Not forgiving self or others requires a great deal of effort. Forgiving is a key component to living a full, rich life. A lot of stories about the power of forgiving are found in the New Testament.

Caring

Matthew 25 is my foundation stone because it tells me what I need to be doing as a Follower: "I was hungry and you gave me food, I was thirsty and you gave me something to drink, I was a stranger and you welcomed me, I was naked and you gave me clothing, I was sick and you took care of me, I was in prison and you visited me" (35–37). There could not be a stronger statement about how I am to show agape to my fellow human beings. Caring about others can add a great dimension to our lives.

One of the more humbling aspects of being a Follower is found in John 13:4–12, where Jesus was eating with his disciples. After supper, he got up from the table, took off his outer robe, and began to wash their feet. Peter objected, but Jesus did it anyway. The story always reminded me that as a priest and a Follower, I am to wash other people's feet, not the other way around. My role as priest is to serve, not be served.

The church talks about agape all the time. So do some of the Old Testament and most of the New Testament. But it is hard to find how one is to practice and implement that love. Situation ethics is the answer, but it is quite different from what many of us have learned. It is one of the most useful tools to help us live life the agape way.

> *The test of Christianity is not about loving Jesus. It's about loving Judas.*
> —Unknown

CHAPTER 7

SITUATION ETHICS

These things I command you, so that you will love one another.
—John 15:17

WARNING: Politically incorrect

An elderly man asked an attractive young woman if she would sleep with him. The woman said, "No, you're too old." The man then asked, "Would you spend the night for $100,000?" The young woman thought a moment and then replied, "Well, yes, for $100,000." Then the man asked her if she would do it for $10,000. She hesitated and then replied, "Probably." His next question was, "How about $100?" The young woman became indignant and shouted at him, "What do you think I am?" The man answered, "We have already established that. Now we're just haggling over prices."

(The above story was told by Joseph Fletcher in the introduction of his book *Situation Ethics*. That was in 1966. In 2023, it is seen as sexist. I included it here because I love to share jokes and had a big collection, but today my collection is down to about 20 percent of the original ones because so many are no longer politically correct. I'm not sure whether this is a good or bad thing.)

Many folks make decisions hoping they are based on their belief system, but that can be a hit-or-miss approach. A better way of decision-making uses agape as its basis, and this methodology can help people make all their ethical and moral decisions. The interesting thing is that often the outcome is not the expected one, but it will always be based on agape. The system is very easy with very few basic guidelines.

We were living in Hawai'i when Rev. Dr. Joseph Fletcher, an Episcopal priest and seminary professor, published a very controversial book entitled *Situation Ethics: The New Morality* (Westminster Press, 1966). This book caused an international crisis; it seemed to undermine the teachings of the church.

Once I heard about it, I wanted a copy, and once I received it, I could not put it down. To me, it was a breath of fresh air that made great sense. (On the other hand, some church folks wanted to try Fletcher for heresy.)

I became a fan of situation ethics (SE). For fifty-five years, I have made my ethical decisions using SE. It has gotten me in trouble (at times, it is contrary to so-called Christian morality), but I still make my decisions based on its parameters.

USING SITUATION ETHICS

Here is an example of SE. A woman in her seventies came to see me as a priest, pastoral counselor, and psychotherapist. I knew the woman and her husband, a physician, as members of our church. They had been married for almost fifty years when he was diagnosed with Alzheimer's. I did not know that her husband had had numerous affairs with his staff and patients and was open about them. Over the years, he had been verbally, emotionally, and physically abusive to his wife. It did not sound like a healthy marriage, but one would never know it from seeing them in church.

As his Alzheimer's progressed, he became more abusive and his family agreed that he should be placed in a nursing home. The couple had four adult children, all of whom were married and lived all over the United States. The children seemed not to be aware of how abusive their father had been to their mother. They were all under the impression that their parents had a lovely marriage and that their father was a wonderful husband and doctor.

Despite the fact that he had been so abusive, every day the woman went to the nursing home to be there with him. Most of the time, he had no idea who she was and they had little or no communication. But she stayed for three or four hours each time.

At the nursing home, she met a man who came regularly to visit his wife. She also was in the advanced stages of Alzheimer's and did not recognize her husband. He still visited her daily. The two visitors started talking and soon became friends because neither had anyone else with whom they could share their feelings and their pain. One day, the man asked my client if she would like to go to the movies, a matinée. She accepted and they went. Afterward, they went to dinner and both realized that a romance had developed. After dinner, they went back to his condo and ended up in bed having sex.

My client shared that she had a wonderful evening and she felt that she was in love with this man. She understood that they had both committed adultery, which was frowned upon by society and the church. She was terribly conflicted because she knew that she had missed the mark (sinned) but also that she had never received that kind of attention and tenderness from her husband.

She asked, "What do you think?" This is where situation ethics came into play.

The foundation stone of SE is the highest form of love, agape. It is also the foundation stone of my belief system and, I think, of Jesus's. It demands unconditional love, accepting people no matter where they are on their life's journey, forgiving them and others, and genuinely caring for everyone. For the practitioner of SE, true justice is simply agape distributed, ascertaining at all times that only the end, agape, justifies the means. The most important point with SE is that every situation is based on the circumstances rather than on the rules, laws, or customs for the so-called morality of a group.

With this in mind, here is what I shared with my client.

First, I acknowledged that she had committed adultery and that the spouses of both my client and her friend were in a near-vegetative state, with eventual death the only option.

Second, the woman's husband seemingly never took his marriage vows seriously. Being married to someone who openly makes a mockery of the institution of marriage is difficult. One cannot forget how abusive he had been to her over the years. Even though they were legally married, in reality they were living a lie.

Third, when I was a child, marriage was supposedly sacred. During my lifetime, I have seen marriage become much less sacred and divorce become comparatively simple, without the stigmas of fifty years ago. "For better or for worse" has become an empty phrase. I have had couples ask me to eliminate those words from their wedding ceremony.

Fourth, I suspect that my client's children would have been opposed to what their mother and this man did. But as far as I was concerned, it was none of their business. They did not know all the facts nor did they need to know. They had not experienced their father's abuse.

Finally, this woman had tolerated bad behavior from her husband for over fifty years. The other man had been a caregiver to his wife for over ten years. They were lonely and exhausted from caregiving. These two people now had a chance to have a loving, caring, sharing relationship. It might not ever happen again.

As long as these two people kept their relationship a secret, no one else in the world needed to know. So what was my advice to this woman? Continue her relationship with this man, do not tell anyone else, do their daily visiting, and be discreet. I know she was very relieved when I shared my thoughts, and as far as I know, the relationship progressed as planned.

SE is a morality that demands that we look at situations individually rather than prescriptively. Laws do not care about circumstances and most have no wiggle room.

Another example of "justifiable adultery" is when seniors live together "in sin" because if they marry, they would both lose Social Security income or other sources of revenue. Often the circumstances, primarily the pocketbook and common sense, suggest that not marrying is the better option.

Some couples live together, have children, and are a family but have never been legally married. For many reasons, they do not feel that a piece of paper makes a marriage. Others do not care what the church thinks and do not want a wedding in one. So many cannot have or do not want an expensive wedding, and a church ceremony can be the start of spending outrageous sums. For some couples, families can be a hindrance and prohibit them from marrying, so they live together. Or their sexual preference prevents them from marrying. What makes a relationship flourish are two people willing to work hard at living together, not a piece of paper or a religious rule.

SITUATION ETHICS IN JESUS'S TIME

Following are some examples, as described in the gospels, where Jesus practiced SE, even though there was no such designation in his time.

In Judaism, at the time of Jesus, it was mandated that one should not touch, much less associate with, anybody deemed a leper. (It seems as if almost any skin condition, such as eczema, psoriasis, or acne, was labeled "leprosy.") Jesus did not seem to care much about the law. He was much more interested in living agape with this detested group of people rather than obeying some law (see Matt. 8:1–4, Mark 1:40–45, and Luke 5:12–16 and 17:11–19). Jesus touched lepers, healed them, treated them respectfully, and ignored the law used against them.

Orthodox Jews were extremely strict and refused to mingle with gentiles. Not Jesus. He mixed with gentiles, he healed them, he went to their homes, and he showed agape to them because in his Kingdom (or is it Kin-dom?) he accepted everyone.

Probably the most famous example of SE was when Jesus met the woman at the well in Samaria. He violated all sorts of rules because the circumstances demanded it:

- Jesus was traveling in Samaria. Jews would never set foot in that territory. The Samaritans and the Jews had hated each other for centuries. Jesus did not care. He traveled in Samaria and related to the Samaritans.
- He spoke with a woman. Jewish men were not supposed to speak with unknown women, much less a Samaritan one.
- The story suggests that this woman had a checkered past, which should have made her even more "forbidden."
- After the encounter, Jesus and the disciples stayed in Samaria a few days to preach agape. Jesus wanted to build bridges, not walls. He loved people, no matter who they were.

In the time of Jesus, women were often treated as property, but Jesus welcomed them into his ministry and gave them positions of authority. Unfortunately, the early male church leaders had no interest in empowering women and made certain that every bit of evidence that supported elevating women was destroyed. That is still happening.

Jesus's ministry was primarily to his fellow Jews, but in Matthew 8:5–13 he heals a Roman centurion's servant and we start to see his ministry reaching out to gentiles, Samaritans, and the Canaanite woman whose daughter was tormented by demons (Matt. 15:22–28). Agape accepts everyone.

Over and over, Jesus exemplified the idea that agape was much more powerful than any law. In Mark 2:23–28, Jesus is reprimanded by the religious leadership because on the Sabbath his disciples were hungry and plucked grain to eat. Jesus reminded the leaders, "The Sabbath is made for man, not man for the Sabbath." The needs of human beings are more important than any law.

Jesus was able to see what the situation and the circumstances were and then based his decisions on them and not some law.

The next time you read the gospel stories, make note of all the times Jesus, even though he had never read Joseph Fletcher's *Situation Ethics*, uses SE to minister to his Followers.

THE ESSENTIALS OF SITUATION ETHICS

Before we move on, allow me to summarize the basic guidelines of SE:

- Agape, and only agape, is the foundation stone of SE.
- Agape is unconditional.
- It demands the acceptance of *every* human being, no matter what. No exceptions are allowed—not one.
- SE does not care whether we like the person or not. Agape needs to be given freely to all.
- Judgment is not allowed.
- Forgiveness, of self and others, has to happen quickly.
- Caring, in a helping way, is mandatory.

One of the great attributes of agape is that it does not tolerate racism, classism, or sexism and does not care about the color of one's skin or a person's sexual orientation, mental condition, political party, finances, disabilities, religious preference, or heritage. Accepting all people, no matter where they are on their life's journey, makes life a great deal simpler and easier.

How about trying your hand at living situation ethics? The next chapter offers some examples about how you can make life-changing decisions using SE with very different outcomes.

The Gospel is less about how to get into the Kingdom of Heaven after
you die but more about how to live in the Kingdom before we die.
—Unknown

CHAPTER 8

WHAT WOULD YOU DO?

For those who want to save their life will lose it and those
who lose their life for my sake will find it.
—Matthew 16:25

Joan's mother walked into her bedroom at 6:00 a.m. and said, "Joan, you need to get out of bed and get ready for school." Joan rolled over and went back to sleep. Her mother returned fifteen minutes later and repeated, "Joan, it's time for you to get out of bed and get ready for school."

Joan replied, "I don't want to go," and pulled the covers over her head.

"Joan, you have to get up and get ready."

"But Mom, none of the teachers like me. I'm not going!"

"That's not true. Get up!"

"None of the kids like me!"

"Joan, that's not true."

Then Joan yelled at her mother, "Why do I have to go?"

Her mother shot back, "Because, Joan, you're the principal."

This joke is funny because I never expected that answer, just like I never expected SE to be my foundation stone in life nor agape to be my way of life. Here is how it happened.

- I began incorporating situation ethics into my life in the late 1960s. It felt right. However, I had not yet concluded that Jesus was about agape. I was still into "he died for our sins," even though I did not believe it. By the 1980s, I had become well-versed in the word *love*; especially as described in the Greek language. I saw it as powerful.
- In the 1980s, with the advent of the Jesus Seminar and the Westar Institute, I felt much freer to question and doubt.
- In the 1990s, I gave myself permission to dismiss the resurrection stories as real. They were metaphors. The power of those stories was *inside* the stories. I had to find it.
- In the early 2010s, I discovered the Jewish tool of midrash thanks to Bishop John S. Spong and the notion that the Bible is best read and understood through "Jewish eyes," which, obviously, I do not have. But I could develop a much deeper understanding of Judaism, agape, metaphors, and the Jewish Jesus, the combination of which has given me the elixir of life.

Situation ethics has allowed me to lead a full, rich life. I have shared briefly how SE works, probably vastly different from how you have been taught to make ethical decisions.

However, the best way of explaining how it works and what the outcomes might be is to share some concrete situations and then have you think about what you, with all your new information, would have done. You may find this very different from what you expected. Because you are a thinker and have new information, you might really enjoy the process. Let's give it a try.

SITUATION 1: ASSISTED SUICIDE

At the age of fifty, Don was diagnosed with multiple sclerosis (MS). He was able to work for a few more years and then he took an early retirement because his MS was progressing. After he retired, he and his wife traveled all over the United States in their recreational vehicle, seeing the country and visiting friends. For ten years, Don was able to function well, but then he needed a cane, then a walker, then a wheelchair, and finally an electric one in which he lived almost full time. The couple purchased an RV that had special accommodations for people in wheelchairs and continued traveling. Don's condition deteriorated further, so his wife started doing all the driving, camp setups, tank filling and emptying, cooking, and a myriad of other duties. His wife was exhausted, so they stopped traveling.

Don began losing the feeling in his legs, arms, and hands, but his brain was still sharp. Next, his wife had to wait on him, as he could do little on his own. He experienced lots of pain. He could live in his wheelchair and take powerful pain meds. However, this was not fun, so Don spoke with a friend who knew a lot about assisted suicide. He also read the book *Final Exit: The Practicalities of Self-Deliverance and Assisted Suicide for the Dying* by Derek Humphry (Dell, 1992). Don had no wish to carry on any longer. He shared with his wife and adult children that he was going to take his life. They all understood and did not want Don to suffer anymore through the final painful stages of MS.

He confided in a friend who had supported others who, because of health issues, wished to die. Don asked him to supervise his suicide, and the friend agreed. Neither Don nor his family were church folks, so he received no opposition from religions that are generally against euthanasia. For about a year, Don had saved many of his pain pills, and he had collected enough to end his life. Don set the day; said his goodbyes to his children, family, and wife; ground his pills; mixed them with applesauce; and consumed them quickly. He fell into a deep sleep and died within a day.

I feel every human being is responsible for his or her life and how to lead it. I do not believe there is a God "UpThere" who has a schedule for when each of us is born, when we are to die, and what we have to do in between. In fact, this is a silly idea. We have absolutely no control over how long we live, but we are responsible for how we do life. I feel we also have a right to say, "I'm finished."

I am a proponent of assisted suicide and look forward to the day we can do it easily and legally.

This is situation ethics.

SITUATION 2: PREMATURE BABY

I had known Sarah since she was twenty years old, when she came to me for counseling. After the therapy was finished, we remained friends. I officiated at her ceremony when she married Michael. A few years later, their first child was born prematurely and lived only a few hours. A couple of years later, their second child was born at twenty-two weeks in the pregnancy. Michael called me and asked me to come to the hospital to baptize the baby. They did not think the baby could survive. I still vividly remember that I could hold the baby in the palm of one hand (and I don't have big hands) as I baptized her. However, baby Emma was a fighter who wanted to live. Emma had thirteen operations on her brain in her first year of life, which caused a great deal of brain damage. In her second year of life, she had three more operations on her brain. Her future looked bleak, but Mom and Dad took excellent care of her and gave her every conceivable opportunity. By the time she was two, it was obvious Emma would never walk or talk or be able to play with other children. But she had a winner smile, which won over everyone.

Sarah had to become a full-time caregiver, which, after a few years, took a toll on the couple's marriage. They went to the state and asked for financial assistance to pay for supplemental help but were told that the only way they could receive any aid was to put Emma in a foster home. The state would not fund the parents directly for in-home help. Sarah and Michael could not believe that such a silly rule existed, but they knew they had to try it. Sarah was able to visit Emma's foster home almost daily, but this was not the same as Emma being in her own home with her parents. Emma started to fail and was hospitalized.

The doctors said that Emma's shunt had to be replaced or she would die. The parents did not want to put Emma through surgery again because they knew more damage would be done to her brain and her life would be even more restricted.

They called me: "What should we do?" We had a long conversation and concluded that with surgery, Emma could live longer but would have no quality of life. The parents faced this reality and decided that they did not want to proceed with the operation and were willing to let Emma die. This was a gut-wrenching decision but the right one, considering the circumstances.

Next issue: Emma was in a hospital that had religious affiliations, and her parents knew the hospital would do everything possible to keep Emma alive, regardless of her prognosis. I suggested, even though it was against the doctors' wishes, that they take Emma out of the hospital and bring her home where they could make the decisions they wanted, not simply accept the decisions the hospital would make.

Knowing these facts, what would you have told Sarah and Michael to do? Keep in mind that we are talking about situation ethics, which looks at every situation differently depending upon the circumstances and makes a final decision based on agape.

What did happen? Sarah and Michael took my advice. Once Emma was home, they knew that she had a limited amount of time left, and unfortunately, her death was predicted to be during the Christmas holidays, making a difficult situation even more difficult. The parents and I spent quite a bit of time together discussing their deepest feelings about allowing their daughter to die. We kept coming back to the same conclusion: Emma would never have any quality of life, and their marriage would be jeopardized. We also spoke about considering adoption in the future because it became obvious that Sarah would have a difficult time having a successful pregnancy.

Some people did not like the parents' decision, but they also did not have a child who needed 24/7 caregiving and had no idea what that entailed. Fortunately, the parents stayed strong and never waffled on their decision to allow Emma to die peacefully at home. Emma lasted until Christmas night, and although her passing was extremely sad, everyone felt a great sense of relief. Now life could move on with new possibilities.

Do you think the parents made the correct decision by allowing Emma to die? Such moral and ethical decisions are challenging, especially since this way of thinking might be new to you. Often the black-and-white decisions that the church usually offers do not look at the circumstances, which often force one to evaluate a decision at a deeper and more understanding level.

Change is never easy!

This is how SE works: every decision is made depending on the circumstances and the power of agape.

SITUATION 3: THE UNWANTED

In our society today, some groups of people, simply because of their "labels" are put into a category I would call "unwanted." Here are a few of them: homeless people; pedophiles; prostitutes; mentally challenged people; sexual offenders; felons; physically disabled people; gang members; gay, lesbian, and transgender people; races other than white; murderers; and observers of some religions.

There are more. Jesus had them in his time: lepers, Romans, tax collectors, disabled people, gentiles, prostitutes, and adulterers, to name a few. However, Jesus accepted and ministered to these people because his kind of love, agape, was unconditional.

As Followers, we, too, are to love people—"all sorts and conditions" (*The Book of Common Prayer*)—unconditionally. True Followers can have no lists. Not only is this part of being a Follower but it also makes life much easier. I have to accept all people, no matter where they are on their life's journey. This is not negotiable.

Let me share a warm and tender story that has a strong message about unconditional love.

Tony, a world-renowned evangelical preacher, had been invited to Hawai'i to preach. Since he came from the East Coast, his body's time clock was six hours off, so in the middle of the night he was wide awake and ready to go to work. At 3:00 a.m., Tony decided to get up and find a coffee shop. Not too far from his hotel, he found an open diner and went in to order a cup of coffee. It was a busy place, even at that hour of the morning.

After he had ordered, Tony noticed a group of women seated behind him. It became obvious that they were "women of the night" who had just finished working. Tony was fascinated that the women were sitting around chatting about their dreams and frustrations as if their lives were no different from anyone else's. He could not help but eavesdrop. One woman stated that her birthday was the next day and that she had never had a birthday party. She explained that her family had been dysfunctional and that she was raised on the streets. Tony had an idea. He would arrange a party for her.

By dawn, the women had all left the restaurant, and Tony went up to the manager and asked if the women came in often. The manager explained that they came every night between 3:00 and 4:00 a.m. and left about dawn. Tony asked if it would be possible to arrange a birthday party for one of the women. The manager said, "Of course. Who's going to pay?" Tony explained that he would cover all the expenses and then he and the manager discussed details.

The next night, the women started to gather as usual. The early arrivals were clued in as to why the restaurant was decorated. The birthday woman arrived and shortly thereafter a cake with lighted candles, flowers, and some gifts were brought to her table. Everyone started to sing "Happy Birthday," and the birthday lady broke down in tears. When she had gathered her wits, she wanted to know who had done this. The manager pointed to Tony in the corner. He walked over, introduced himself, sat down with the women and enjoyed some cake. The birthday woman, with tears streaming down her face, gave Tony a huge hug and a kiss on the cheek. She told him it was the nicest thing anybody had ever done for her.

This is a sentimental story, but is also agape at its best. Tony crossed all sorts of barriers to honor and recognize a human being who was a victim of the ills of society. Tony gave this woman dignity by accepting her as she was and perhaps giving her new perspective on life, even if only for a moment.

Jesus does this over and over, giving people, especially those who are on the "unwanted" list, new life, not judgment and rejection.

SITUATION 4: TAKING THE HIGH ROAD

Mike went to work as a project manager for a large manufacturing company. Within two years, he had brought in so much business that the company promoted him to vice president, overseeing sales for the entire division. He worked closely with a coleader, and they were able to bring a marginal group into their division to become the third largest in the entire company, with annual revenues in the hundreds of millions.

When Mike's coleader retired, he was replaced by an authoritarian man, Ray, who micromanaged everyone through bullying and intimidation. He seemed to have a propensity to alienate one and all, resulting in many managers and staff transferring to other divisions. The morale was terrible and this division gained the reputation of being an undesirable place to work. Sales declined. When contracts developed problems, Ray's only method of dealing with the issues was to harass and denigrate people.

Mike found it difficult to work with this man. He spoke with higher management, but no one wanted to listen. As Mike saw it, he had three choices: (1) stay where he was and tolerate Ray; (2) transfer to another division in the company, taking a pay cut and demotion; or (3) leave the company and try to find a new job in a down economy.

What do you think you would have done if you were in Mike's situation? Here's what actually happened.

Mike was a faith-based person who could no longer tolerate Ray's "leadership." He also knew job-hunting during the current economic downturn was going to be challenging.

Mike had shared all of his struggles with his wife. She knew that Mike always took the high road and that he would not be happy staying. Fortunately, she had a job that could tide them over until he found meaningful work.

Mike shared the story with me. I knew Mike. He had high ethical standards, and he had to leave. This is agape. It demands high standards, and regardless of the consequences, one always has to take the high road.

This was not the first time I saw Mike living his faith. In an earlier incident, Mike and a group of church friends decided to start a company. It was doing very well until a down market wiped them out. Unfortunately, the five owners had just taken out a big loan from a bank. Four signers of the loan simply walked away from it. Mike, however, could not; he took full responsibility for the entire loan and, after years of frugal living, paid off the loan.

Followers always have to take the high road. Agape demands it.

SITUATION 5: RACISM

I thought the election of Barack Obama as president of the United States in 2008 was a turning point in our country and proof that maybe we had risen above racism. It was pivotal but, unfortunately, in a negative way. It proved that racism was much deeper than many imagined.

In 2016, the Electoral College chose an open racist as the next president of the United States. Almost half of our country concurred.

Racism has permeated every facet of our country. Some of it is subtle, but a great deal of it is out in the open, blatant, and violent. How do we deal with this issue creatively?

As a Follower and believer that agape is the answer, there can be no racism. We are to love everyone unconditionally.

Years ago when agape became my foundation stone, I knew that I needed to do some introspection about my own racism. I knew it was there. As I dug down, I realized my racism is alive and well. Earlier I confessed that I am a recovering racist. Now it is subtle, but in the past, my racism was much more in the open.

I cannot eradicate that I was a white boy raised in a Black neighborhood where name-calling and fighting were part of my growing up. And even though I was only eight years old at the start of World War II, I believed it was patriotic to hate the Japanese, the Germans, and the Italians, our enemies.

As a child and teenager in the church, I learned that the Jews killed Jesus. I did not know anyone who was Jewish, but I still called Jews nasty names and was antisemitic.

I am a veteran of the Korean conflict and have negative images and used derogatory language about the Korean culture.

It is important for me to recognize that I am a recovering racist and even at my age realize that I shall never be a recovered racist. My racism will always be there, maybe deep down but still within. Fortunately, agape, unconditional love for everyone, neutralizes my racism and demands that I be pro-active with those who use racial slurs or tell racist jokes.

We had some casual friends over at our house for dinner. One of the women, who had had too much to drink, started using the n-word and making derogatory remarks about Black people. This is unacceptable. I was polite but forthright and told her, "I feel uncomfortable when you use that word and make those kinds of remarks about Black people. Please don't do it in our presence." This approach can stop some people in their tracks.

A little later, after this guest had more wine, she started using racist slurs again. One more time, I had to be confrontational. I reminded her that this makes us uncomfortable. With that, she suggested that it was time for her to leave. She left and so did our other guests. End of gathering.

This is situation ethics in action. Agape is the foundation stone of SE, and I feel as Followers we must always stand up for unconditional love no matter what because this love has no room for racism, sexism, misogyny, homophobia, classism, elitism, or any other negatives concerning people.

Currently, the institutional church continues to emphasize salvation rather than agape. What is the future of the church? Following are some options. One is utopian but doable. The second is realistic and provocative. The third is guaranteed to close the doors of churches. Which of these churches do you or would you attend?

Christianity has always been an evolving story. It never was a finished story.
—Bishop John Shelby Spong

CHAPTER 9

I Can Dream, Can't I?

So faith, hope, love abide, these three; but the greatest of these is love.
—1 Corinthians 13:13

A car was moving at 22 mph in a 35 mph zone. A policeman saw it as a hazard and pulled the car over. There were five elderly men in the vehicle. The driver was very alert, but the other four men looked like zombies, very pale and seemingly frozen in place. The policeman explained to the driver that he was pulling him over because he was driving 22 in a 35 mph speed zone and he was a hazard. The man replied, "But officer, the sign back there said 22." The officer replied, "Sir, that is a route sign. You are on route 22. I'm going to let you go, but please drive the speed limit. However, I have a question: What is wrong with your four friends? They are pale and zombie looking." The driver replied, "I have no idea, but we just came off route 119."

(Sometimes I feel that so many of my progressive ideas make people think that they have just come off route 119.)

Do you ever wonder if the institutional church has a future? Fewer and fewer people are going to church or giving it much credence. Some folks think if the church switches from being a salvation machine to an agape machine (being an instrument to change the course of civilization through agape), the church might have a long future. This process could be a long one because people need to be convinced that the Great Commandment is the key to a better world. However, if

65

people are given the opportunity to question, doubt, and discuss the church's future in a neutral climate, everyone can grow, change, and evolve, resulting in individual and institutional change.

My evolution includes a dream that the church will also evolve. The title of this chapter—"I Can Dream, Can't I?"— is from a song written in 1937 and made famous by the Andrews Sisters in 1949. I can still remember it as a slow, snuggly dance number that was most popular in my late high school and early college days. I use it as a title for this chapter because I want to share my dream of how to make the church relevant in the twenty-first century.

I think most churches are aware, at some level, that the institutional church in the United States and throughout Europe has died or organ failure is occurring and it is only a matter of time. I have heard estimates that over four thousand churches a year are closing their doors. I like to say, "Too many, but not enough!" which means too many churches refuse to change and not enough are starting to develop new ways of ministering. Here is an example. Many downtown churches are having to close for lack of money and people. An idea: keep the churches open as agape community centers whose primary task is to minister to homeless people, those living below the poverty level, local businesspeople, and seniors, and offer a myriad of other services to help people living there flourish. This is living Matthew 25:40, doing this for "the least of these."

THE IMPOSSIBLE DREAM?

In an ideal world, this is what I wish would happen:

1. The institutional church admits that it is in trouble and is willing to make drastic changes in its theology, mission statement, architecture, liturgy, and institutional structure.
2. The church recognizes that God is not one-size-fits-all. God is a man-made concept and has many different images depending upon the Believers' interpretation. My dream urges the institutional church to find this acceptable and even to encourage members to question and doubt. This allows Followers to reimagine their image of God as they go through life. Too many churches feel the need to control, which always eliminates questioning and doubting.
3. The church recognizes that its complex, outdated, sometimes silly theology is not important. Most of the time, people do not attend church because of its theology but because they like its mission statement, the pastor is a good preacher, or they like the fellowship.
4. The church brings back the historical Jesus—the real man and his real message—and lets go of the Jesus who is the son of some god who lives UpThere or the son of a god who planned his son's torture and death. We need to let go of the idea that someone died for our sins and we do not have to be responsible for our mess-ups. We need to let go of a Jesus who is perfect (there is no such thing) and talks to us. He has been dead for almost two thousand years and does not

talk—especially in American, an English dialect. The Jesus who will change the world, as well as you and me, is the historical one whose constant message was agape, unconditional love of all.

5. The church adopts a mission to minister to the hurting world 24/7. This is the agenda that is going to attract millions of people to an institution that has the power to transform people's lives. Wars, incarceration, segregation, injustice, and a caste system (including in America) are no longer acceptable. Our energy is now directed toward a path that helps people move forward so that they can be all they were created to be. This is when the church becomes THE CHURCH. (There is a huge difference.)

I realize that most of the above wishes have next to no basis in reality. Some people might call them "crazy," but as the title of this chapter suggests, "I can dream, can't I?"

I am not sure, at the age of ninety plus, how much more time I have on this earth, but I know that I still have enough time to plant seeds as to where the church of the future needs to go.

Enough of the dreams. Here is a possible reality.

A POSSIBLE DREAM

The following scenario is still in the "dream" category but perhaps has a more realistic approach. These ideas are shared more for those who have a progressive mindset.

I think most progressives know that the future of the institutional church is nebulous. They know that the church needs to make some radical changes but have no idea or limited ones about how to make this happen. As a pastor, I know that what we learned in seminary is not what the people in the pews (with their checkbooks) think. Too many resist change.

Following are some ideas to start the ball rolling:

1. I suspect that the hierarchy in the institutional church knows that the church is in trouble and needs to make changes, maybe radical ones. Perhaps we should stop reminding the church that it must change or die and just leave that elephant (the declining church) in the middle of the room, pretending it is not there.

2. In the past, the church has been rather good about changing things by purposefully not discussing a subject. For example, as a child growing up, I heard about the Blessed Trinity all the time. Today one hardly ever mentions it, which is fine with me. It has never made any sense no matter how many times someone tried to explain it. I always ended up with three different gods, which was not the idea behind the doctrine of the Trinity.

I feel the same way about almost all the theology of the church. As a priest, theologian, member of a specific group (Episcopalian), and teacher-preacher, I have an obligation, according to my Episcopal ordination, to defend the faith. My best way of defending the faith is not to talk theology. Therefore, I ignore issues about Immaculate Conceptions, virgin births, the Trinity, predestination, heaven, hell, purgatory, the real presence (the doctrine that the bread and the wine are the real body and blood of Jesus), divine intervention, judgment, life after death, Jesus as the Son of God, literal interpretations of miracles and the resurrection stories, and almost any theology the church has. They mean so little to me in my daily living. I often see them as divisive and irrelevant. So let's stop talking about them and soon they will become nonissues.

3. I am always hesitant to define God. Thousands of concepts exist about who or what God is, and since they are all inventions of man, I do not think it is worthwhile for us to spend time on who is right or wrong. My own definition has changed numerous times. For the early part of my life, God lived UpThere, tended to be meaner than a junkyard dog, and ran earth, and maybe the universe, with an iron fist. Early in my ministry, I switched from *God* to the word *Creation*. No one seems to have a problem with that, or the phrases *Ground of All Being* or *Higher Power*. I am still good with *Creation*.

   Your definition of God is just as valid as mine because it is what we believe now. I hope my definition keeps changing as I go through life.

4. Without a definitive theology and no definitive God, I am now able to see Jesus in an entirely different light. No longer is he the Son of NoOneUpThere who died for my sins and arose from the dead but simply a historical human being. This means he was a real person with a realistic transforming message about agape. Agape is the foundation stone of my life. I do not need any highfalutin theology with a bunch of fancy unpronounceable words to describe who Jesus was. I see him as a prophet or sage who was the right person at the right time with the right message. Interestingly, the message was not really his. He simply quoted from his Jewish Pentateuch (the first five books of the Old Testament) using these words: "You shall love the Lord your God . . . [and] your neighbor as yourself" (Matt. 22:37–39). He was talking about unconditional love that forgives quickly, accepts everyone, and cares about others.

5. The major task of this dream church is to minister to the hurting world. Donating money is helpful and writing letters challenging political and economic systems is fine, but I think the biggest mission is a hands-on, I-Thou relationship: helping refugees resettle, demanding first-class medical care for people who have mental health disorders (including those suffering from addiction), supporting prison reform and helping inmates going through rehabilitation, helping people escape poverty, providing homes and services for the homeless, offering tutoring services to young people so they do not drop out of school, and demanding high quality medical services for all who live in this country.

No longer can the church be an extension of the country club whose members gather on Sunday morning to sit in the comfortable pews and hear sweetness and light. The future church has to regain its title of being the arms and hands, feet and legs of the body of Jesus, physically dead but alive in spirit and demanding that we demonstrate agape to "the least of these."

Let me share some thoughts from the presiding bishop of the Episcopal church, the Most Reverend Michael Curry. Because I am minimally involved in the Episcopal church, I do not stay abreast of its happenings. But I had heard that in 2015, the Episcopalians had chosen their first Black bishop, from North Carolina, to be the number one bishop in the church.

I next heard of him when Annie and I were driving from New Hampshire to Chicago visiting family and friends, and our car radio was tuned to the wedding of Prince Harry and Meghan Markle. All of a sudden, Bishop Curry came on and his preaching style was not that of staid Episcopalians. It was more like a revival meeting and his message was powerful, all about the power of love.

In October 2019, Annie and I were in Hawai'i, where I was doing some preaching, teaching, and working with homeless people. A special meeting was scheduled in Honolulu for all Anglican clergy in the Pacific basin, and since we had heard that Bishop Curry was going to preach at the Cathedral of St. Andrew that evening, Annie and I attended. His speaking style is electrifying, and once again he preached about love being the answer to man's needs. His sermon was powerful.

The following year, the bishop's newest book, *Love Is the Way: Holding on to Hope in Troubling Times* (Avery, 2020) was published. Let me share this portion of his book: "I can't speak for other religious traditions, but the further Christianity has strayed from its roots in Jesus of Nazareth—his teachings, his example, and the reality of his risen life—the more we have betrayed the one we claim to follow. . . . When the way of love becomes one's way of life, it's a game changer. It shapes every decision we make—and that changes everything, whether you're a preacher or a politician, a communist or a corporate executive, a teacher or a trash collector. And it cannot be limited to just the personal. Once it's your spiritual center of gravity, it floods every aspect and dimension of life" (pp. 229–230).

For me, this is the essence of life, living agape. Then, throughout the gospels, Jesus clearly defines how I am to lead my life. This makes Jesus my Christ because I know if I do what he tells me, my life will be transformed and most fulfilling. I also know that this is the message for all Followers.

If we keep these ideas in mind, then perhaps we can see that a more realistic approach to changing the direction of the institutional church is to preach, teach, and indoctrinate all those who want to follow this Christ to establish churches (meaning groups of people, not buildings) in which they practice agape—for themselves, for other members of the church, and for the hurting world.

In this new reality, church structures no longer need to conform to medieval concepts of what a church should look like but become more of a community center that is open and welcoming to one and all. The objective of the center is to minister to the hurting world. The members of this church become the legs, feet, arms, and hands of Jesus. He has already told us in Matthew 25:40 what we are to do. Now let's do it.

Years ago, I was reminded by a wonderful man in Ecuador, my Spanish professor, that the name of Jesus is an action verb, not a passive noun. Believing in Jesus demands action, agape action. I really like that concept.

Some of these agape churches will have a paid pastor, while others will be run by volunteers. One does not have to belong to the church to volunteer. One simply needs a desire to do positive things for the hurting world.

Is this too easy and too simple? It might sound that way, but believe me as a social worker and one involved with social action for my entire adult life, this is not easy because we live in a complex world and ministering, especially to the hurting world, is challenging.

A few agape churches already exist, and any church that sees this as the wave of the future has many great examples to follow. I can guarantee any church that seriously follows this path will flourish and be fulfilling not only the Great Commandment but also the powerful words of Jesus as stated in Matthew 25:40, "inasmuch as you have done it unto the least of these, you have done it unto me."

MY NIGHTMARE

Now I will share my ideas of what I see as the future for conservative churches, those churches that have little or no interest in change. I am not sure how long they are going to survive. Change in general in the twentieth and twenty-first centuries has been astronomical, and it does not seem to be slowing down. But if institutions do not change with the times, they die. When I was a child and young adult, Sears, Roebuck and Company was a powerful merchant. In 2021, it barely exists. It could have changed but refused. To me, this is analogous to those mainstream churches that refuse to change. They seem to be closing lots of their doors.

But I am not willing to give up on them. My plea, echoed by Bishop Curry, Bishop Spong, the Westar Institute, and many progressive clergy and churches, is that every church look into the power of agape love. But this is almost impossible to do if one is homophobic, misogynistic, racist, sexist, or resistant to change. If conservative churches do not see Jesus as the purveyor of unconditional love, forgiveness, and acceptance of anyone and everyone no matter what, then they are going to find it exceedingly difficult to continue much longer, unless they have a huge endowment. Their days are numbered.

It was interesting for me in 2020 to look at the protests happening around our country. George Floyd was murdered by the people who were supposed to be protecting him and us. When I watched the protests and saw hundreds and thousands of young people with great diversity in race, creed, and background, it gave me a profound hope for the future of this country and the world.

When I was a young adult and a young priest, the institutional church was the moral compass for our country. It started schools, universities, hospitals, homeless shelters, orphanages, runaway shelters, homes for unwed mothers, and community centers. But now that the institutional church is in survival mode, it has almost given up outreach to the hurting world and its influence in society and culture is almost nonexistent.

Being Followers of Jesus and devotees of agape, we can transform ourselves and the world to become game changers in how we do life in the twenty-first century.

This is my wildest dream: that this book is provocative enough to stir some people and maybe a church or two to use it as a conversation starter to make changes. The next chapter offers some suggestions on how to begin your evolution.

People can't see what they can't see, unless someone helps them.
—Brian McClaren

And thus, this book.

CHAPTER 10

POSSIBLE WAYS TO USE THIS BOOK

And Jesus increased in wisdom and in years, and in divine and human favor.
—Luke 2:52

A fourth-grade girl was talking with her teacher about whales, and the teacher stated that it would be impossible for a human to be swallowed by a whale. The girl mentioned that the Bible says Jonah was swallowed by a whale. The teacher, a bit irritated, reminded her that it would be physically impossible, to which the girl said, "When I get to heaven, I'm going to ask Jonah." The teacher said, "Suppose Jonah is in hell?" The little girl replied, "Then you ask him."

There could not be a safer place to experiment than a progressive church where one discusses Jonah being swallowed by a whale and what is going to happen after we die. Our congregation's motto, "No matter who you are or where you are on life's journey, you are welcome here," means we are free, without judgment, to try new things, rejecting some and accepting others. But whether you belong to a church or not, let's look at how you might start your leap into evolving and transforming.

Let's start with a question. If you go to church, why? Here are some possible responses:

- I enjoy fellowship with like-minded folks.
- I like the church's theology or mission statement.
- It is a lifelong habit.
- I like the clergypeople.
- I feel comfortable with my church friends and pastor.
- I want to grow in my faith.

The last reason might pose a challenging task. Here are some things people have told me about growth and change.

- Change is not easy for me.
- Why change? My belief system seems to have worked for me for many years.
- Certain childhood messages—for example, "The Bible is inerrant," "I am a sinner," "I am a bad person," "Don't question, don't doubt"—are hard to overcome.
- If I change, someone will be very unhappy or angry with me.
- I was told not to question or doubt the church, its teaching, or its ministers.
- If I do question or doubt, something terrible will happen to me.
- The constant threat that if I doubt or question, then when I die, I will go straight to hell.
- No one ever gave me permission to doubt or question without severe consequences.
- If I don't do what the church tells me, I'll be excommunicated.

Let me reassure you, none of the above statements are true. Jesus spent his life questioning and doubting Jewish leadership. See Matthew 23.

SOME SUGGESTIONS ABOUT HOW TO USE THIS BOOK

If you want to grow in your faith, start small and don't jump ahead in the process. This could be a big change in your life, and it is best done with the mentoring of a Progressive Christian. I have written a workbook to help you through this process.

Some recommended first steps follow:

1. If you're working by yourself, slowly make your way through each exercise in the workbook. If you have a problem understanding something, review the suggested readings at the end of each chapter of the workbook. You may also email me at bilaulenbach@yahoo.com and I would be happy to help you.
2. Read and do the exercises along with a friend. This will allow you to share your ideas with each other.

3. If you are a member of the clergy, use this book as sermon material for a four- or six-week series. Have the workbook available for church members who would like to do the exercises after you preach a sermon based on a chapter or a couple of chapters. You may make copies of the workbook if you like.

4. Use this book as a four-week Advent or Lenten program. When I teach classes, I always have a daytime (usually morning) session followed by an evening session using the same materials. This allows people who have to miss one session to be able to hear the material in another session. There are two interesting outcomes. The first is that people can stay involved, and the second is that most of the time we have very different conversations even though we use the same materials.

   I can assure you of this: this book is provocative and will stimulate thinking as well as allow people to share their thinking. This always promotes growth in your church family.

5. For university/college professors who are interested in Progressive Christianity, this book will provoke conversations as well as help younger people come to grips with their own belief system.

Here are some other ideas:

1. Start by learning about the Gospel of Mark, the first gospel written and the easiest to read. Before you read it, go to Wikipedia and look up "Gospel of Mark." Read the background materials as to when the gospel was written, who wrote it and why, and for whom it was written.

2. Now read the Gospel of Mark. It is easy to read, and most scholars think it served as the foundation for Matthew and Luke but not John. Stop at Mark 16:8, where the gospel originally ended. Notice that there is no resurrection story. Much later, a redactor added Mark 16:9–20, a resurrection story. The important point: a human being (or beings), Jewish, wrote the gospel, not a god nor a Christian. The Gospel of Mark, or any other gospel, is not a historical history. It is a religious history that is not interested in the facts about the actual life of Jesus but the truths found inside the stories the writers told.

3. Next, look up the word *midrash*, which means "biblical interpretation." Midrash is an extremely important process to learn to discover the truths within the gospels.

4. As you read this gospel, start trying to determine what the writer says about Jesus. Who was Jesus according to Mark?

As you can see, the process of thinking progressively can be a long, slow, tedious, and maybe even painful one. (Mine was painful for many reasons.) For me, this process has taken some sixty-plus years, partly because I did not have permission from the hierarchy or anyone to guide me for thirty years.

Taking time to define who God is or isn't to you right now is helpful because your definition (there is no right or wrong answer) will make a difference in how you investigate Scripture. The image of an old white man living above the third tier of the flat earth in his many mansions is not going to get one very far in the twenty-first century.

It is probably way too early in the process for you to accept that God is a man-made concept. There are many steps in between.

Whatever stage you are in, please do not stop praying.

SOME CLOSING THOUGHTS

Growing in your faith is a slow process that should not be hurried through. Time is on your side, so go slowly!

A mentor can help you move through this process successfully. Choose a mentor whom you trust.

At the beginning, you might feel out of control, perhaps accompanied by anxiety and fear. That is because you are slowly eradicating the old to make room for the new. Often you might feel like there is a vacuum—because there is. Be patient! Slowly but surely, we are going to fill that vacuum with new beginnings.

You are not the first person going through this process. It started for me in seminary as the old was eradicated, making room for the new. My bishop made me promise not to leave seminary before the end of the first year. He was correct to do so. I thought about leaving at least a half-dozen times. The process was scary, but I had seminary staff who understood it and supported me. This is probably the most important advice I can give you: hang with the process. I suspect you experienced similar feelings with your first car, your first job, your first love, your marriage, and all the other challenges you faced while growing up and evolving.

Remember, take one little step at a time and learn to be comfortable with that step.

Pray every morning for strength, patience, and understanding. Express gratitude for being able to take your faith to a new level.

One of the hardest parts of this is not praying to NoOneUpThere. The church keeps telling us that we are the hands and feet of Jesus. No longer can we give NoOne a list of all the things she or he needs to do this week. You and I have to do those jobs. Remember: there is NoOneUpThere (except two to four trillion galaxies). I believe you will find that all the jobs you used to give God to do are overwhelming and maybe, now that you need to do them yourself, you will understand why the old form of prayer is not what to "do to the least of these." In the workbook, I give many more details about how one prays when there is NoOneUpThere.

I can guarantee that as you question, doubt, grow, evolve, and transform, you will lead a life richer than you ever imagined in your wildest dreams.

Never before did I understand how fulfilling and meaningful constant transformation could be, has been, and still is in my life.

In closing, I'd like to share my daily prayer (I call my God *Creation*):

May all the colors of Creation give me a sense of awe and wonderment.
May Creation be a sacred presence within me.
May Creation be a source of inspiration and courage.
May Creation keep pulling me forward.
May Creation go with me on my journey today and continue to bless me.

No, I didn't write this, and I have no idea from whence it cometh, but it centers me every time I say it.

How To Make Love

(The Agape kind)

with Jesus

WORKBOOK

Preface to the Workbook

To live life to the fullest, one has to keep evolving, even at ninety years old. For me, evolving means questioning, changing, growing, and transforming. This workbook is designed to help you do that. Please note that page numbers in parentheses in this workbook refer to page numbers in the main text of the book.

If you consider yourself a Progressive Christian (PC), you might use this workbook to evaluate where you are in the wide spectrum of PCs. For example, I label myself as extremely progressive, maybe even a heretical progressive.

If this is your first foray into the progressive world, you might find the exercises in this workbook terribly threatening, and perhaps you will not be able or even willing to complete them. If that's the case, I'd like to suggest that you just do one or two of the exercises to get an idea of what being progressive might mean. In no way am I trying to convert you, suggest that you are wrong, or push you into anything you aren't ready to do. As Rabbi St. Paul suggests, you have to "work out your own salvation with fear and trembling" (Phil. 2:12–13).

The process of moving into the progressive world is not easy. It demands changing, eradicating old ideas, and experiencing a sense of emptiness. It is like learning any new skill: it will take time, patience, frustration, and maybe even guilt for leaving behind the old and familiar as well as friends and starting a new chapter. Although it is not easy, I can assure you that moving through this process is going to open new possibilities in your life that you never imagined.

If you are already a PC, this workbook can help you see where you are now and maybe encourage you to keep moving to the next step.

My own life has changed radically since becoming a PC. Every morning when I get up, I know exactly what I have to do, and then I spend the day doing it. So far, in my ninety years, I have been able to confront every situation life has thrown my way because I know what I have to do to resolve it. I have been married to the same wonderful woman for over sixty years, primarily because Progressive Christianity has given us the tools to move through challenges and conflicts.

As a Progressive Christian, I don't have to carry any negative baggage. It is all resolved. Almost on a daily basis, I find new information that influences my thinking and my being a PC. Regardless of my age, I know that I'll be able to keep moving forward and progress throughout the rest of my life.

Thank you for reading this workbook and for being interested in growing "in wisdom and stature and in favor with Creator and humanity" (Luke 2:52).

INTRODUCTION (See pp. 1-11)

WHERE DO WE START?

I want this workbook to be thought-provoking and not a tool to go through as quickly as possible. Take your time responding. No one else will see your answers, so be honest. For most questions, there is no right or wrong answer, just what you think at that moment.

THE PROCESS OF EVOLVING (p. 2)

Desire to Evolve (p. 3)

■ Do you have a desire to change and evolve? Why or why not?

_____

_____

Ability to Think (p. 3)

■ Are you willing to put your critical thinking hat on? Why or why not?

_____

_____

Interest in Listening (p. 3)

■ Are you good at listening? Explain your answer.

_____

_____

■ Do you want to improve your listening skills? Why or why not?

_____

_____

Desire to Transform Oneself (p. 4)

■ Are you ready to start transforming your life now? Why or why not?

_____

_____

WHAT DO ALL THOSE WORDS MEAN? (p. 4-10)

The point of the following exercise is to allow you to see how your thinking has progressed (or maybe digressed) over the years. Suggestions: (1) skip words you don't know, and (2) be honest, even if you think you might look foolish. You have already received an A+ for tackling this workbook.

agape (a-gah-peh) (p. 5)

■ Have you heard the word *agape* before? When and where?

_____

_____

■ Do you like the concept? Why or why not?

_____

_____

god, GOD, or God (p. 5)

■ Who, what, and where was your God when you were about twelve years old?

_____

_____

■ What about today?

_____

_____

Jesus (pp. 5–6)

- Who was Jesus to you when you were twelve years old?

_____

_____

- What about today?

_____

_____

Christ/christ (p. 6)

- Do you have a Christ?

_____

_____

- What or who is he/she/it?

_____

_____

Holy Spirit (p. 6)

- Who or what was the Holy Spirit (Ghost) when you were twelve years old?

_____

_____

- What about today?

_____

_____

Bible (pp. 6–7)

- What does the Bible mean to you?

_____

_____

■ Who do you think wrote it?

_____

_____

midrash (p. 7)

■ Have you ever heard of the word *midrash* or been introduced to the biblical interpretation process? When and where?

_____

_____

■ Does it make sense to you? Why or why not?

_____

_____

"Saint" Paul (pp. 7–8)

■ What is your opinion of Paul?

_____

_____

Nativity stories (p. 8)

■ Which Nativity story do you like best and why?

_____

_____

virgin births (p. 9)

■ Do you believe that translating a word from Hebrew to Greek could make a young woman a virgin? Why or why not?

_____

_____

Resurrection (p. 9)

- Do you believe in a physical resurrection of a dead body? Why or why not?

  _____

  _____

- Could you believe that these resurrection stories might be metaphors? Explain your answer.

  _____

  _____

dogma, doctrine, and tradition (p. 9)

- What is your favorite theology?

  _____

  _____

- Do you dislike any theology? If so, which one and why?

  _____

  _____

miracles (p. 10)

- Do you believe the biblical stories concerning miracles are true? Why or why not?

  _____

  _____

life after death (p. 10)

- Do you believe in a life after this one? Why or why not?

  _____

  _____

- What do you think is going to happen after you die?

  _____

  _____

church versus Church (p. 10)

◼ Do you understand this difference?

_____

_____

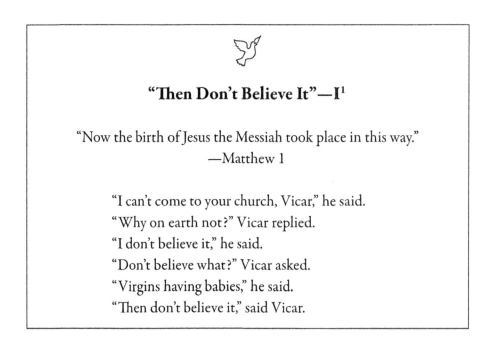

> ### "Then Don't Believe It"—I[1]
>
> "Now the birth of Jesus the Messiah took place in this way."
> —Matthew 1
>
> "I can't come to your church, Vicar," he said.
> "Why on earth not?" Vicar replied.
> "I don't believe it," he said.
> "Don't believe what?" Vicar asked.
> "Virgins having babies," he said.
> "Then don't believe it," said Vicar.

SUGGESTED READINGS

Daily Life at the Time of Jesus (2007), by Miriam Feinberg Vamosh.
Dictionary of the Daily Life and Times in Biblical and Post-Biblical Antiquity (2014), by Edwin M. Yamaguchi and Marvin R. Wilson.
Honest to God (1963), by John A. T. Robinson, an Anglican bishop who upset the status quo.
Into the Whirlwind: The Future of the Church (1984), by Bishop John Shelby Spong.
On Being a Christian (1974), by Hans Küng, a former Roman Catholic priest. This book started me on my road to being "progressive."
The Once and Future Faith (2011), by Robert W. Funk and others. Funk is the founder of the Westar Institute and a member of the Jesus Seminar, a group of over two hundred Biblical scholars, historians, linguists, archaeologists, professors, and researchers.

Bishop Spong has written twenty-nine books and Robert Funk at least nine books.

---

[1] Adapted from "Nativity" by Rev. David Keighley in his book *Poems, Piety, and Psyche*, p. 75.

UNDERSTANDING AGAPE

I believe this chapter is the heart of Jesus's message, so it is ever so important to understand these keywords.

TYPES OF LOVE (pp. 14–16)

- Have you had an agape experience where you demonstrated love and expected nothing in return? Describe your experience.

_____

_____

AGAPE DAD (p. 16)

If you're not familiar with the parable known as "The Prodigal Son" (which I prefer to call "The Father Who Showed Agape"), you can read it in its entirety in Luke 15:11–32.

- Who are you closer to in giving love: the dad or older son? Explain your answer.

_____

_____

■ Do you believe there can be any exceptions to agape love?

_____

_____

■ If so, who do you think should be an exception and why?

_____

_____

■ Read the following statement: As soon as any person or religion puts one condition (e.g., gays cannot marry) on agape, that person or religion becomes a cult or cult member hiding behind the robes of religiosity to substantiate their prejudices. Do you agree or disagree with this statement? Explain your answer.

_____

_____

AGAPE IN ACTION (pp. 16–17)

Another parable, "The Good Samaritan," should be called "Agape in Action." It can be found in Luke 10:25–37.

■ How does this story demonstrate "agape in action"?

_____

_____

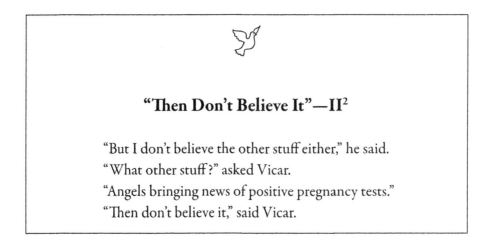

"Then Don't Believe It"—II[2]

"But I don't believe the other stuff either," he said.
"What other stuff?" asked Vicar.
"Angels bringing news of positive pregnancy tests."
"Then don't believe it," said Vicar.

[2] Adapted from "Nativity" by Rev. David Keighley in his book *Poems, Piety, and Psyche*, p. 75.

SUGGESTED READINGS

The Acts of Jesus: What Did Jesus Really Do? (1998), by Robert W. Funk and the Jesus Seminar.

The Gospel of Jesus, 2nd ed. (2014), by Robert W. Funk and others. This short book is about what Funk and the scholars of the Jesus Seminar believe are actual words from the mouth of Jesus or at least very close.

Introducing Christian Ethics: Core Convictions for Christians Today (2021), by David G. Gushee. I am pretty sure that if Jesus were around today, he wouldn't believe how complex his basic message of agape has become.

The Jewish Annotated New Testament (2011), edited by Amy-Jill Levine and Marc Zvi Brettler. Levine is Jewish and a professor of the New Testament at Vanderbilt Divinity School. This book also has sixty-nine fascinating articles in the back of the book.

The Once and Future Jesus (2000), by John Shelby Spong and others.

The Oxford Dictionary of the Christian Church, 3rd ed. (2005), edited by F. L. Cross and E. A. Livingstone. Primarily use this book to look up words that interest you. Otherwise, if you have trouble sleeping, I suggest you put this book by your bed and when you wake up in the middle of the night, start reading it from cover to cover. Sleep will come quickly. But it is a good reference book.

The following three books are products from the Westar Institute, a very progressive organization:

The Complete Gospel Parallels (2012), edited by Arthur Dewey and Robert J. Miller.

The Complete Gospels (2010), edited by Robert J. Miller. This book also includes the gospels found in the Dead Sea Scrolls, Nag Hamadi Library, and other sources.

The Five Gospels: The Search for the Authentic Words of Jesus (1993), by Robert W. Funk and others. This book also includes the Gospel of Thomas and shows how the Jesus Seminar voted on these writings as to whether they were the authentic words of Jesus.

CLARIFICATIONS

Words and their meanings are ever so important, so I need to make certain that you understand these five concepts. They come into play a great deal, especially when we are dealing with situation ethics (SE).

AGAPE LOVE VERSUS LIKE (p. 20)

■ What's the difference between liking someone and loving unconditionally?

_____

_____

■ Could you show agape to someone you do not like?

_____

_____

TOUGH LOVE (pp. 20–21)

■ Can you do tough love? If not, why not?

_____

_____

INDIFFERENCE (p. 21)

■ Have you ever been indifferent to someone? If so, describe the circumstances.

_____

_____

CONSCIENCE (p. 22)

■ Do you think your conscience should be your guide? Why or why not?

_____

_____

JUSTICE (pp. 22–23)

■ Do you believe there is a difference between moral justice and the justice one sees in the US legal system? Why or why not?

_____

_____

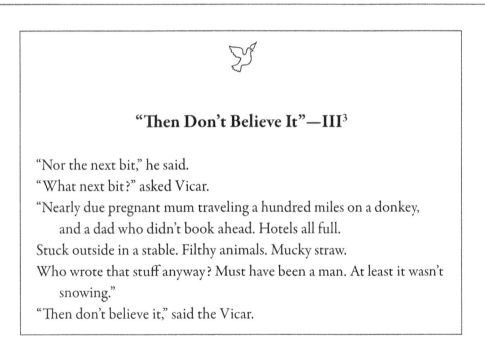

"Then Don't Believe It"—III[3]

"Nor the next bit," he said.

"What next bit?" asked Vicar.

"Nearly due pregnant mum traveling a hundred miles on a donkey, and a dad who didn't book ahead. Hotels all full.

Stuck outside in a stable. Filthy animals. Mucky straw.

Who wrote that stuff anyway? Must have been a man. At least it wasn't snowing."

"Then don't believe it," said the Vicar.

---

[3] Adapted from "Nativity" by Rev. David Keighley in his book *Poems, Piety, and Psyche*, p. 81.

SUGGESTED READINGS

Days of Awe and Wonder: How to Be Christian in the 21st Century (2017), by Marcus J. Borg.

Liberating the Gospels: Reading the Bible through Jewish Eyes (1997), by John Shelby Spong.

Unbelievable: Why Neither Ancient Creed nor the Reformation Can Produce a Living Faith Today (2018), by John Shelby Spong. The bishop died before this book was finished, but his wife, because she was so involved with his thinking and writing, was able to finish it.

Why Religion? A Personal Story (2018), by Elaine Pagels, a progressive thinker and writer.

CHAPTER 3 (See pp. 25-30)

CONFUSERS

I have found that there is much confusion as to what the primary message of Jesus was and what it wasn't. For the Follower of the Way, she or he must be able to clarify it quickly or this concept will not make sense.

- What do you consider the ruling norm of Christianity?
  - ☐ The Ten Commandments
  - ☐ The Golden Rule
  - ☐ I don't know
  - ☐ The Beatitudes
  - ☐ The Great Commandment

- Explain your answer.

  _____

  _____

THE TEN COMMANDMENTS (pp. 26–28)

- Do you follow the laws found in the Ten Commandments? Why or why not?

  _____

  _____

THE GOLDEN RULE (p. 28)

■ Do you use the Golden Rule as a guideline in your life? Why or why not?

_____

_____

"I DON'T KNOW!" (pp. 28–29)

■ Why do you think people say "I don't know" when they are asked what Jesus's main message was?

☐ They have an answer but are not sure it is the response the asker wants to hear.

☐ They have never thought about this issue.

☐ A stock answer comes to mind—"Jesus died for my sins" or "Jesus is God or His Son"—but they feel safer saying, "I don't know."

☐ They have an answer but fear people might think it is stupid.

☐ Other. Explain: _____

_____

THE BEATITUDES (p. 29)

■ Do you think it is possible to live by the standards set in the Beatitudes? Why or why not?

_____

_____

THE GREAT COMMANDMENT (pp. 29–30)

■ Do you think it is possible to live only by the Great Commandment? Why or why not?

_____

_____

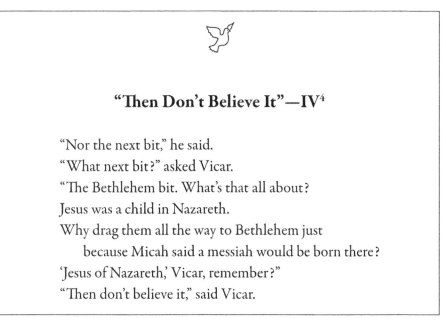

"Then Don't Believe It"—IV[4]

"Nor the next bit," he said.
"What next bit?" asked Vicar.
"The Bethlehem bit. What's that all about?
Jesus was a child in Nazareth.
Why drag them all the way to Bethlehem just
    because Micah said a messiah would be born there?
'Jesus of Nazareth,' Vicar, remember?"
"Then don't believe it," said Vicar.

SUGGESTED READINGS

Reading the Bible Again for the First Time: Taking the Bible Seriously but Not Literally" (2001), by Marcus J. Borg.
This Hebrew Lord (1993), by John Shelby Spong.
Jesus for the Non-Religious (2007), by John Shelby Spong.
How to Read the Bible and Still Be a Christian (2016), by John Dominic Crossan, a former Roman Catholic priest.

---

[4] Adapted from "Nativity" by Rev. David Keighley in his book *Poems, Piety, and Psyche*, p. 84.

THE PROBLEMS WITH
A DEAD MAN WALKING

The idea that Jesus died for our sins has been so ingrained in the institutional church that I suspect a majority of Christians will see this chapter as pure heresy. Thus, the following explanations are very important to enumerate as others "fight" you about this thinking.

TIMING (pp. 32–33)

- Do you believe that the stories of Jesus might have changed during the time between the death of Jesus and the first writing of Mark? Why or why not?

_____

_____

LACK OF CONSENSUS (p. 33)

- Do the differences among the resurrection stories trouble you? Why or why not?

_____

_____

TWENTY-FIRST CENTURY (pp. 33–34)

■ Do you think science and technology are threats to the church? Why or why not?

_____

_____

DEATH (p. 34)

■ Do you believe that Jesus actually rose from the dead? If so, how do you account for the rapidity and by-products of bodies decaying?

_____

_____

SITZ IM LEBEN (pp. 34–35)

■ If you know how the Romans carried out crucifixions in Jesus's time, how does that affect your belief in the resurrection stories?

_____

_____

SIGMUND FREUD (pp. 35–36)

■ Do you agree with Freud that religion is infantile? Why or why not?

_____

_____

SPACE EXPLORATION (p. 36)

■ Do you think it was possible for Jesus to ascend into space two thousand years ago? Why or why not?

_____

_____

MIDRASH (pp. 36–37)

■ Which, if any, of the above subjects in this chapter elicited a reaction, negative or positive? Explain your answer.

_____

_____

KEEP QUESTIONING

Remember: No subjects are off limits. All questions and doubts are encouraged. (How else can we grow?) What you think now is always valid. I have no interest in changing anyone's theology, politics, or point of view. I do have a strong interest in giving you a platform to ask your questions and exchange ideas without fear of being wrong, ostracized, or put down, making you feel your thoughts are heretical.

■ Do you have any questions about Jesus and the resurrection stories? If so, write them here and then find answers from a PC.

_____

_____

_____

_____

Do you want to discuss your ideas but do not have anyone with whom you feel comfortable doing that? Contact me at bilaulenbach@yahoo.com. I love to listen and share ideas. Or I would be happy to refer you to another Progressive Christian whom you might have more in common with.

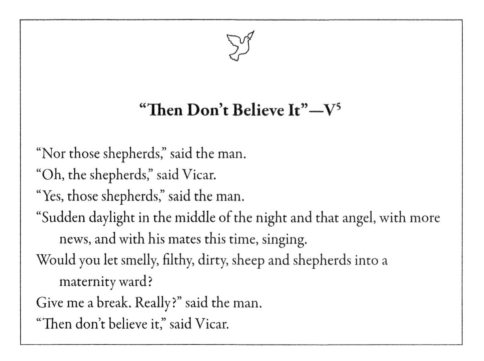

"Then Don't Believe It"—V[5]

"Nor those shepherds," said the man.
"Oh, the shepherds," said Vicar.
"Yes, those shepherds," said the man.
"Sudden daylight in the middle of the night and that angel, with more
    news, and with his mates this time, singing.
Would you let smelly, filthy, dirty, sheep and shepherds into a
    maternity ward?
Give me a break. Really?" said the man.
"Then don't believe it," said Vicar.

---

[5] Adapted from "Nativity" by Rev. David Keighley in his book *Poems, Piety, and Psyche*, p. 86.

SUGGESTED READINGS

Does God Exist? An Answer for Today (1978), by Hans Küng.

The Easter Moment (1980), by John Shelby Spong.

The Last Week: What the Gospels Really Teach about Jesus's Final Days in Jerusalem (2006), by Marcus J. Borg and John Dominic Crossan.

Resurrection: Myth or Reality? (1994), by John Shelby Spong.

The Resurrection of Jesus: A Sourcebook (2001), edited by Bernard Brandon Scott.

The Trouble with Resurrection (2010), by Bernard Brandon Scott.

Who Killed Jesus? Exposing the Roots of Anti-Semitism in the Gospel Story of the Death of Jesus (1995), by John Dominic Crossan.

CHAPTER 5 (See pp. 39-44)

THE POWER OF THE RESURRECTION— AS A METAPHOR

Thinking of the resurrection as a metaphor has transformed my life. Nothing else I learned in church or in seminary or in the real world has been as powerful in my ninety years. I hope you can understand the concept, use it as part of your daily living, and see and feel tremendous changes in your lifestyle.

■ Is the idea of the resurrection stories being metaphors versus being true stories new to you? If so, how do you feel about the concept?

_____

_____

SEEING THE GOSPELS FROM A NEW PERSPECTIVE (pp. 40–42)

■ Do you understand the concept of midrash, the Jewish way of interpreting scriptures and sharing your truths? Why or why not?

_____

_____

■ How does midrash help in showing you that the truth of the resurrection is found in the story, not the story itself?

_____

_____

OTHER EASTER STORIES (pp. 42–44)

■ Do you have a personal Easter story? Please briefly describe it here.

_____

_____

_____

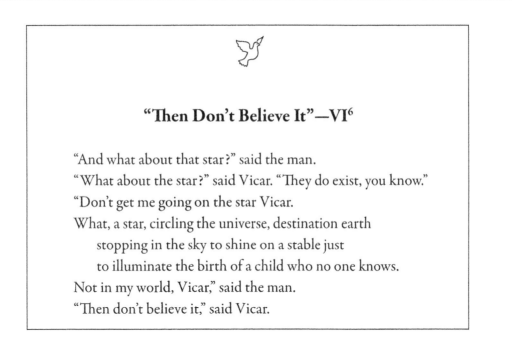

"Then Don't Believe It"—VI[6]

"And what about that star?" said the man.
"What about the star?" said Vicar. "They do exist, you know."
"Don't get me going on the star Vicar.
What, a star, circling the universe, destination earth
    stopping in the sky to shine on a stable just
    to illuminate the birth of a child who no one knows.
Not in my world, Vicar," said the man.
"Then don't believe it," said Vicar.

SUGGESTED READINGS

Biblical Literalism: A Gentile Heresy: The Journey into a New Christianity through the Doorway of Matthew's Gospel (2017), by John Shelby Spong.

The Heart of Christianity: Rediscovering a Life of Faith (2003), by Marcus J. Borg.

Jesus: A Revolutionary Biography (2009), by John Dominic Crossan.

Jesus Reconsidered: Scholarship in the Public Eye (2007), by Bernard Brandon Scott.

Midrash: Reading the Bible with Question Marks (2013), by Sandy Eisenberg Sasso.

---

[6] Adapted from "Nativity" by Rev. David Keighley in his book *Poems, Piety, and Psyche*, p. 89.

It's about Love

Now let's consider what the New Testament has to say about agape, forgiveness, and the resurrection metaphor.

PAUL (pp. 46–47)

■ Do you agree with the idea that laws would not be needed if all of us practiced agape? Why or why not?

_____

_____

AGAPE BIBLICAL QUOTES FROM OTHER WRITERS (pp. 48–49)

Judging (p. 48)

■ Do you consider judging others good or bad? Explain your answer.

_____

_____

■ What can you do to help yourself minimize (or eliminate) the number of times you judge others?

_____

_____

Forgiving (p. 48)

- Do you find it difficult to offer forgiveness easily? Why or why not?

_____

_____

Caring (pp. 48–49)

- In what ways do you demonstrate care to other people, including strangers?

_____

_____

PRAYING

For years, people have been praying to a God whom I call NoOneUpThere. Prayers in Christian churches, in public settings, and in private spaces are full of telling NoOne what to do, pleading for mercy and help, and even damming NoOne for not doing what was asked.

- Do you pray? If so, how often?

_____

- What do you do when you pray?

_____

_____

- Is your prayer life satisfactory? Explain your answer.

_____

_____

For forty years, I have seen prayer as a way to do a series of actions:

1. Be thankful for all Creation and each day to remember specific items in Creation (the sun, a bird, the sky, or maybe a warm sun or a cool breeze).
2. Make a daily list of the people and things for which I am thankful.

3. Make a list, which changes almost daily, of specific people who are facing challenges in life. On a daily basis, I contact one or two of those people by phone, email, or text or in person to let them know I am thinking of them, hoping they are finding the strength to heal, to forgive, to endure. (Churches do this by sending demands or messages to NoOneUpThere and hoping She/He/It will take care of it.)

4. Remember my shortcomings, not only in the previous twenty-four hours but also in my life. I need to make certain that I have forgiven myself and others. Not forgiving is like drinking poison and waiting for the other person to die.

5. Make a list of the things I want to do every day to make this a better world in which to live.

■ Would you be able to change your prayer life or style? Why or why not?

_____

_____

■ I have given you a model I have followed. Does it make any sense to you? Explain your answer.

_____

_____

■ What might you add or change to suit your own prayer style?

_____

_____

"Then Don't Believe It"—VII[7]

"And how do three kings get in on the act?" asked the man.

"Wise men, you mean?" said Vicar.

"Have you seen a Christmas card lately, Vicar?" asked the man.

"Three kings on camels,

trekking across the hills, day and night,

only for the magic star to get them lost in Jerusalem.

'Find the king,' cries Herod, sending them off to search.

Why search? What's happened to the magic guiding star?

And led, do you get this, led—by a star! To Bethlehem, where it stopped!

Stopped, Vicar! Stopped in the sky. Brian Cox will be apoplectic.

Where they give a brand-new baby gold and perfume and herbs. What!

And if the baby grew up poor, Vicar, what happened to the gold, eh?

Tell me that?

Really Vicar, too much communion wine?"

"Then don't believe it," said Vicar.

SUGGESTED READINGS

The Fourth Gospel: Tales of a Jewish Mystic (2013) by John Shelby Spong.

The Jewish Gospel of John: Discovering Jesus, King of All Israel (2015), by Eli Lizorkin-Eyzenberg.

The Power of Love: Sermons, Reflections and Wisdom to Uplift and Inspire (2018), by Michael Curry.

---

[7] Adapted from "Nativity" by Rev. David Keighley in his book *Poems, Piety, and Psyche*, p. 92.

SITUATION ETHICS

This chapter is the "how to" portion of this workbook. It is your chance to practice making SE decisions, all based on agape. You might find this methodology very different from how you have made your decisions in the past. I hope you have fun doing it as well as learning a new life skill.

In the book (p. 52), I shared the story of a woman in her seventies whose abusive husband had Alzheimer's and lived in a nursing home. While visiting him, she met a man whose wife also had Alzheimer's and no longer recognized him. Imagine she came to you for advice about her relationship with this married man.

■ What might you have said to this woman?

_____

_____

■ Would you call her an adulteress? Why or why not?

_____

_____

■ Was she wrong or immoral? Explain your answer.

_____

_____

■ Can you see any justification for this woman's having committed adultery? Explain your answer.

_____

_____

■ What is your opinion of my thinking (p. 53)? Does it irritate you or make you angry, or are you sympathetic?

_____

_____

SITUATION ETHICS IN JESUS'S TIME (pp. 54–55)

■ Can you think of an example when Jesus seemed to ignore the laws of his time and instead practiced his version of situation ethics? If so, briefly describe it here.

_____

_____

THE ESSENTIALS OF SITUATION ETHICS (p. 55)

■ Since agape is the foundation of situation ethics, what does SE say about racism, classism, sexism, and discrimination based on skin color, sexual orientation, mental condition, political party, finances, disabilities, religious preference, or heritage?

_____

_____

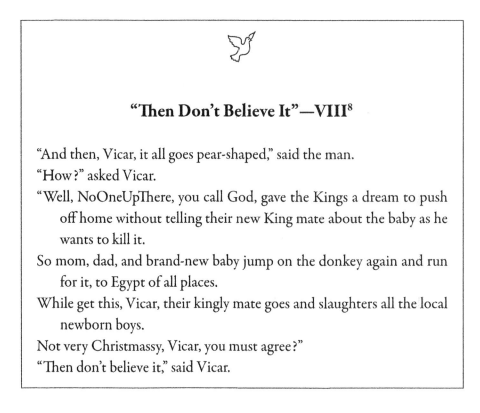

"Then Don't Believe It"—VIII[8]

"And then, Vicar, it all goes pear-shaped," said the man.

"How?" asked Vicar.

"Well, NoOneUpThere, you call God, gave the Kings a dream to push off home without telling their new King mate about the baby as he wants to kill it.

So mom, dad, and brand-new baby jump on the donkey again and run for it, to Egypt of all places.

While get this, Vicar, their kingly mate goes and slaughters all the local newborn boys.

Not very Christmassy, Vicar, you must agree?"

"Then don't believe it," said Vicar.

SUGGESTED READINGS

Situation Ethics: The New Morality (1966), by Joseph Fletcher.

Situation Ethics: The New Morality (1998), by Joseph Fletcher, edited by the Library of Theological Ethics.

Situation Ethics: A New Look at "The New Morality"! (2019), by Ralph Montonaro.

See Amazon for more books dealing with ethics.

---

[8] Adapted from "Nativity" by Rev. David Keighley in his book *Poems, Piety, and Psyche*, p. 94.

WHAT WOULD YOU DO?

This chapter includes more SE exercises. Several situations are described in the book that are not repeated here. I encourage you to review pages 57–64 and use those examples for discussion. The following stories are new exercises, each dealing with a different situation.

SITUATION 1: ADULTERY

This story takes place at the end of World War II and is set in Berlin. Early one morning as Mrs. Bergmeier was out foraging for food for her three children, she was picked up by a Russian patrol and immediately taken to a prison camp in Ukraine. Her husband had been captured in the Battle of the Bulge and taken to a prison camp in Wales. Mrs. Bergmeier had no way to let her children know what had happened.

Finally, her husband was released and returned to Berlin, where he spent weeks looking for his family. He was able to round up two of their children: Ilse, twelve, and Paul, ten. They were found in a detention school run by the Russians. The oldest boy, Hans, fifteen, was later found hiding in a cellar near the Alexanderplatz. Their mother's whereabouts remained a mystery, but they never stopped searching. She, more than anything else, was needed to reunite the family in their dire situation of hunger, chaos, and fear.

Meanwhile, in Ukraine, Mrs. Bergmeier learned through a sympathetic Russian commandant that her husband and children were trying to find her. She also learned that prisoners could be released for two reasons:

1. Illness: Any prisoner needing medical facilities beyond the camp's capabilities would be sent to a Soviet hospital elsewhere.
2. Pregnancy: The woman would be returned to Germany as a liability.

She turned the second alternative, becoming pregnant, over in her mind. Yes, she would try that. She asked a friendly prison guard to impregnate her, which he did. She knew that she was committing adultery, a grave sin, and that the newborn child would be labeled as illegitimate. She also knew that she had a much higher motive, agape, to be reunited with her family.

As soon as her condition was medically verified, she was sent back to Berlin, where she was able to locate her husband and children. She shared her story with her family and was still welcomed with open arms. When the child, named Dietrich, was born, the family loved him, understanding he was the bridge that reunited the family.

When it became time for Dietrich to be christened, the parents went to the church and had Dietrich baptized. After the ceremony, they sent the children home and sat down in the pastor's study, shared all, and asked if they should be grateful to the prison guard. Had Mrs. Bergmeier done a good and right thing?

Unfortunately, too many folks would be judgmental (agape has no room for that) and label Mrs. Bergmeier as an adulteress and little Dietrich as a bastard.

This case is built on understanding the circumstances. The sexual act to conceive the baby was based on Mrs. Bergmeier's decision to do the most loving thing possible to be able to return to her family.

The closest example in the ministry of Jesus I can find is the story of Jesus saving the adulterous woman from being stoned to death (John 7:53–8:11). The circumstances, other than the woman having committed adultery, are different but Jesus's reaction was similar to Mrs. Bergmeier's family's reaction. He accepted the woman even though she had sinned.

SE's first concern always is agape. Mrs. Bergmeier's only intent was to become pregnant so that she could be reunited with her family. It was a chancy, courageous act that could have gone wrong in so many ways.

The circumstances surrounding the birth of Dietrich remained a family secret, and Dietrich had a birth certificate showing Mr. and Mrs. Bergmeier as his parents.

This is how SE works. Agape is always the end, although sometimes the means can be deemed immoral by some. For me, SE has made my life much easier because I always understand what it is I have to do: agape. I simply have to figure out the means to make that happen.

- How do you feel about the Bergmeier family's situation?

  _____

  _____

- Was Mrs. Bergmeier an adulteress? Why or why not?

  _____

  _____

- Is what she did evil or bad? Why or why not?

  _____

  _____

- Was baby Dietrich a bastard? Why or why not?

  _____

  _____

  _____

  _____

SITUATION 2: DIVORCE AND REMARRIAGE

In the Old Testament book of Malachi, the prophet claims the God of Israel said, "I hate divorce" (2:16). I am not sure anyone believes divorce is fun, but in the twenty-first century, I see it as a necessary alternative to an unhealthy marriage.

Jesus allegedly also had some strong words about divorce and remarriage. In the Gospel of Mark (10:11–12), he states, "Anyone who divorces his wife and marries another commits adultery against her." Matthew adds, "except for immorality" (Matt. 5:32, 19:9). That is very straightforward. I would call it black and white without any gray. I believe that life has a lot of gray.

Before retiring, I was a psychotherapist (licensed clinical social worker) and spent a great deal of time dealing with marriage and divorce. In so many situations, it seemed that divorce was the best choice in a series of negative options. I could never tell a woman to stay in her marriage if her husband continually beat her up physically or emotionally. Most of the time, couples came to me after their marriage had been a shambles for years. It is extremely difficult for people to stay in a marriage after many years of unresolved negative baggage. If minor children are involved, it is not fair to drag them through the tension of two unhappy, angry adults living under the same roof.

My methodology, if people were willing (not many were), was to have a separation so that the couple would not live in the same quarters. I also suggested that I see the husband and wife separately so I could hear what each person had to say without the other person being there. If that worked, then I suggested that the couple start dating on a limited basis. Once we saw how that progressed, I then pushed for the couple to get back together or see a divorce attorney or mediator.

I have always felt the church came down too hard on divorced couples, and in my early ministry I saw the institution as unloving and unforgiving in its refusal to allow divorcées to be remarried in the church. Divorced people have been through hell and back. They don't need more judgment. They need forgiveness, total acceptance, and lots of caring. (This sounds like agape.) Bottom line: I was always ready to remarry people in either a church setting or a private venue.

Before officiating at a marriage where there had been a previous divorce, I would spend extra time with the couple because I discovered, over the years, that people tended to remarry the kind of person from whom they had divorced. I even offered Divorce Recovery Workshops to help people deal creatively with their lives after a divorce.

This story is about Sam (sixty-five) and Karen (fifty-two), who wanted to be married in the church. Karen had never been married, but Sam had previously been married three times and had been single for the last twenty years. At first, the couple wanted the rector to officiate at a small wedding in the church. Because the church has lots of rules about being remarried in the church, the rector insisted that Sam write all the details about his previous marriages and then present them to the diocesan bishop for his judgment. Sam had no interest in regurgitating those unhappy moments in his life. He was also told by the rector that even after going through this exercise, the bishop still could say no.

So the couple asked me if I would perform the wedding ceremony from *The Book of Common Prayer* in their home with only Sam's son and daughter-in-law being present. I said I had no problem officiating as long as the couple came to see me for premarital counseling. They agreed to that, and after three sessions I felt strongly that Sam had learned from the past and was willing to enter this marriage with a fresh perspective.

I believed Sam and Karen had a good chance of making their marriage work as long as they both worked diligently at being married. I agreed to perform the ceremony knowing full well that I was violating my ordination vows, going against the bishop and the divorce laws of this diocese. I also knew that this couple would probably leave the church if I did not officiate. I felt the church's approach to remarriage had too much legalism and not enough agape. If the institutional church does not accept all people no matter where they are on their life's journey, then that church needs to go out of business. Jesus was about unconditional love, not legalism and rejection.

■ If Sam and Karen had come to you instead of me, what would you have said and done?

_____

_____

My choice was easy. In the name of love, I married this couple. They stayed members of the church and had a good marriage for a number of years. Unfortunately, Sam chose alcohol over a strong marriage and eventually they divorced.

I feel some of the church's laws about divorce are heartless. My first allegiance is always to my Christ and agape.

SITUATION 3: TOUCHY ISSUES

Certain issues in our twenty-first century world keep on being issues because either religion in general or some institutional churches in particular keep throwing fuel on the fire. If religion and the churches backed off, I strongly suspect they would not be issues. Probably the most obvious one is human sexuality. As a child, I was told there are only two types: men and women. In junior high school, I learned that some people were called "homosexuals," and they were males who were sexually attracted to other males. We had pejorative names for them and "knew" they were all bad people. As a young teenager, I had no idea what *homosexual* meant but was careful not to show any traits that one might consider effeminate. In those days, the church was very antihomosexual and many churches still are. The term *gay* had not yet surfaced.

The church also supported the notion that women are second-class citizens. I remember learning as a youth that females could never be much more than teachers, secretaries, or nurses. Because women were labeled "not capable," they were not allowed to make decisions about their bodies. So males made the rules about whether a woman could use birth control, be raped, be beat up, or have an abortion. A group of "neutered" old men in Rome said no to abortions. Other men implied that if a woman was provocative in any way, rape was permissible, and if she was not submissive, beating her up was acceptable. The church also fostered the idea that a woman should be submissive to her husband. Then women realized how much power they had and started telling men that they wanted to be in charge of their life, their sexuality, and their decision-making. Some churches have made great strides, but too many of them still want to keep women suppressed.

Another touchy issue in twenty-first century America is that too many churches dislike and distrust science and promote ridiculous ideas, such as that the world was created seven thousand years ago by their god in six days and then everyone went to church all day on the seventh.

I could go on with more examples, but I think my point has been made: too many religious groups in many Christian churches want to control our lives and the best way to do that is to control our thinking. This approach seems to work, so many people allow their religion or church to tell them how to act and what to believe. If anyone deviates, that person is removed. Unfortunately, one cannot practice situation ethics and belong to these religions or churches because SE says every situation is different and demands different responses as long as the foundation stone is agape. SE does not like rules.

One of my touchier issues is when a religion or church claiming to be Christian makes strong negative judgments about people who are different. At one point, in the name of agape, I tolerated them (barely) but no longer. Also, I do not think Jesus would have. He was strong when it came to challenging people's judgmental behavior. My test as to whether someone is a true Follower centers in that person's total acceptance of all people no matter where they are on their life's journey. There can be no lists, no referring back to the Bible (written two to four thousand years ago), and no relying on outdated traditions to reject anyone.

Jesus tells me that my *neighbor* includes every other human being. This standard makes my life much simpler because now I do not have to have any lists of people that some religion or church suggests are not equal in the eyes of their bigoted cult.

Here is a touchy but real situation that demanded SE. Mary had been a longtime friend of our family as well as a member of one of my parishes. Mary left home, went to college, graduated, and went out into the working world, where she did fairly well. Unfortunately, she became involved in a fundamentalist church that would not fully accept anyone who was not heterosexual. Mary bought into their claptrap and gave me some of it when she said that she loved the sinner (a person who is not heterosexual) but not the sin, which meant she would love so-called sinners as long as they were celibate and did not wish any position of authority in the church. This is conditional love.

I reminded her that we live in a much different world from Paul when he made his great pronouncements against homosexuality. Many scholars believe that Paul's homophobic remarks referred to pagan temple prostitution, where young boys were readily available to older men. But we shall never know.

I also told her that science has shown us that there are many varieties of human sexuality. Some lists suggest twelve different varieties, but I strongly suspect there are ten times that many. Almost daily, authorities on human sexuality add a new type to the list. I also told her our sexuality is not a choice. It is who we are, but some folks are not able to even figure that out.

Mary was not going to budge. Her homophobic church now controlled her mind and closed it to reason. I felt that I no longer wanted to be a friend to Mary. I find that her kind of thinking kills gay and transgender people and puts a scarlet letter on anyone and everyone who is not heterosexual. This does not mean that I do not love Mary in the agape sense of the word, but it means I no longer want to be around her. My situation ethics allows me to make that determination.

My faith also makes it imperative that I challenge people's thinking and speaking when they use pejorative terms about other people's race, creed, sexual orientation, or disability. SE demands that I challenge intolerant people who make statements or tell jokes that denigrate any other human being. (This has played havoc with my joke telling.)

- ▪ What do you think of the stance I took with Mary?

  _____

  _____

- ▪ Would you find it difficult to challenge another person's prejudicial thinking? Why or why not?

  _____

  _____

My Christ, Jesus, made, according to Matthew 23, many strong stances against his Jewish religious authorities because of their biases and bigotry. But that does not mean he did not show them agape.

SITUATION 4: BABY OUT OF WEDLOCK

A woman took her family's secret to the grave. Her younger sister, then ninety years old, almost did also. When she was a teenager, her older sister became pregnant and had a baby out of wedlock, which in those days was a terribly negative event and most of the time kept as a big, dark family secret. The baby was given up for adoption.

The world has changed radically, and now many people have babies out of wedlock and feel no shame. Sometimes a single woman who still wants to be a mother will have a child. Nowadays when a young woman becomes pregnant, society, for the most part, accepts that and supports her without demanding marriage. Many couples do not believe in the institution of marriage but go ahead and have children. Today having children out of wedlock is hardly a stigma.

Back to the story: the ninety-year-old sister, on her deathbed, felt that her family's secret should no longer remain a secret, so she shared it with her daughter. I think the daughter wished she had not been told because then it became her problem. Had she not been told, there would not be an issue. But now she had to choose: keep this secret a secret or share it with her cousins? Wisely, I believe, she chose to pass the secret on to a trusted cousin, who then had to decide what to do with it.

Through extensive DNA testing, the daughter and cousin were able to find their long lost relative. They knew she was alive but nothing else. They chose not to make contact.

Was this a right and good thing?

SE says the daughter handled this situation very well. She took the secret from her mother, shared it with her cousin, who shared it with her siblings. Everyone then had to make their own decision about the relative. From my vantage point, the family did the most loving thing for everyone concerned. They had to do what they felt best for them in their lives.

■ Do you agree or disagree with my opinion? Explain your answer.

_____

_____

SITUATION 5: UNWANTED CHILD

Maria was thirty-three years old and married to Greg, who loved sports. They were his life. The couple had two daughters, ages six and eight. Maria also was a sports fan, and she enjoyed going to sporting events with her husband. Unexpectedly, Maria became pregnant. She was afraid to tell Greg because he had made it crystal clear that parenting was not his thing and he didn't want more than two children. Maria had strong feelings against having an abortion and felt caught. Finally, she shared the news with Greg. He was adamant: an abortion was necessary. Maria could not do it. Greg started going to sporting events with his buddies, leaving Maria at home with their girls. He was extremely angry with her, which caused a great deal of tension in the house. Maria decided to continue with the pregnancy, hoping that once Greg saw the baby he would change his mind.

When Maria was in her sixth month of pregnancy, Greg came home from work and announced that he had been to an attorney and was filing for a divorce. He told Maria that her continuing with the pregnancy indicated to him that this unwanted child was more important than their marriage. He wanted out. Maria was devastated and came to me for advice.

■ What would you have told her?

_____

_____

What happened?

Maria had a healthy baby boy. Greg had finalized the divorce and refused to see the baby or have anything to do with Maria. He felt this baby was responsible for destroying his otherwise good marriage.

I had told Maria early in her pregnancy that she had to reconsider her stance concerning abortion or risk losing her husband. I believe Maria gave Greg no choice because she knew very well his stance about having more children. Maria was wrong to sacrifice her marriage, her children, or their future for the sake of a fetus that had the potential to be a life but at that time was simply a fetus, not able to survive on its own. I spoke about agape, unconditional love, which makes decisions based on doing the most loving thing for the greatest number of people. In this case, her decision to have the unwanted baby adversely affected Maria, her marriage, her children, and probably dozens of family members and friends who would be negatively impacted by a divorce.

Let me share some thoughts about the "forever" issue of abortion. I feel this remains a much talked-about issue because the fundamentalists and the Roman Catholic church keep making it so. Neither group is interested in logic or facts.

Here is where I have problems:

1. Many religions have a great need to control their members. Freethinkers are not welcome. I believe all human beings have to be responsible for their decisions and what they do with their body. I want my religion to give me the tools to make appropriate decisions based on circumstances, not make those decisions for me.

2. Most fundamentalists and Roman Catholics are against abortion because they claim it destroys a life. However, many of them are for the death penalty, taking a life. That does not make any sense to me.

3. It is primarily men who insist on telling women what to do with their lives and bodies because they consider women inferior. In reality, many men are threatened by women's strength, so they only pretend they have the wherewithal to make important decisions.

4. I do not think a human life starts at conception. Life starts, but it is not a child, which then makes me wonder, "If that fetus is a human, why don't we have a funeral service and full burial for all miscarriages?" I have never heard a good answer.

5. Laws against abortion do not stop abortions. Women can still buy a pill, pay a doctor, or use more barbaric methods.

Agape and SE say that every woman has to make that decision for herself, based on her unique circumstances, and be willing to live with it for the rest of her life.

■ What do you think about the issue of abortion?

_____

_____

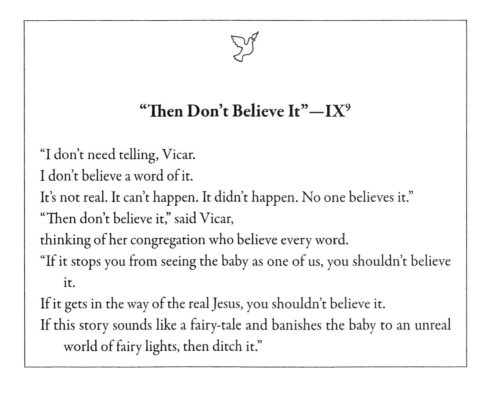

"Then Don't Believe It"—IX[9]

"I don't need telling, Vicar.
I don't believe a word of it.
It's not real. It can't happen. It didn't happen. No one believes it."
"Then don't believe it," said Vicar,
thinking of her congregation who believe every word.
"If it stops you from seeing the baby as one of us, you shouldn't believe it.
If it gets in the way of the real Jesus, you shouldn't believe it.
If this story sounds like a fairy-tale and banishes the baby to an unreal world of fairy lights, then ditch it."

SUGGESTED READINGS

The advice columns Dear Abby and Ask Amy include unbelievable episodes of situations demanding an ethical response.

The Best of Dear Abby (1989), by Abigail Van Buren.

---

[9] Adapted from "Nativity" by Rev. David Keighley in his book *Poems, Piety, and Psyche*, p. 96.

I CAN DREAM, CAN'T I?

Maybe there will be an institutionalized church of the future, depending on what it considers to be its message and mission. I am offering some ideas and want your input. The agape theme could be the thrust—and I am hoping it is. *You* will decide that.

THE IMPOSSIBLE DREAM? (pp. 66–67)

■ Why do you go to church?

_____

_____

Note: In this workbook, I do not include fundamentalist churches, which often call themselves "evangelical," because I see them more as cults or clubs that have rather long lists of those who are not acceptable, read the Bible literally (it was never written to be interpreted that way—ask any Jewish scholar), demand that everyone think and vote alike, and are extremely judgmental.

■ What is your reaction to my stance on fundamentalist churches? Remember, there is no right or wrong answer. These are your feelings, never to be negated.

_____

_____

A POSSIBLE DREAM (pp. 67–70)

■ What would the institutional church look like in your ideal future?

_____

_____

■ Do you think Jesus is a noun or action verb? Explain your answer.

_____

_____

MY NIGHTMARE (pp. 70–71)

■ What do you see as the future of the institutional church if it refuses to change and remains on its current path?

_____

_____

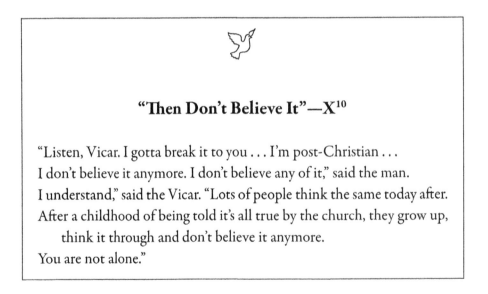

"Then Don't Believe It"—X[10]

"Listen, Vicar. I gotta break it to you . . . I'm post-Christian . . .
I don't believe it anymore. I don't believe any of it," said the man.
I understand," said the Vicar. "Lots of people think the same today after.
After a childhood of being told it's all true by the church, they grow up,
    think it through and don't believe it anymore.
You are not alone."

---

[10] Adapted from "Nativity" by Rev. David Keighley in his book _Poems, Piety, and Psyche,_ p. 99.

SUGGESTED READINGS

Future Church: Seven Laws of Church Growth (2020), by Will Mancini and Cory Hartman.
Rebooting Church: The Future of Church (2019), by Walter Franklin Davis.

See Amazon for more books dealing with the church and the future.

POSSIBLE WAYS TO USE THIS BOOK

This could be the start of a new transformed, love-centered life. I hope you might have the opportunity to experience it.

In the previous chapter, I asked "Why do you go to church?" Here are some possible responses:

- I enjoy fellowship with like-minded folks.
- I like the church's theology or mission statement.
- It is a lifelong habit.
- I like the clergypeople.
- I feel comfortable with my church friends and pastor.
- I want to grow in my faith.

The last answer might pose a challenging task because it requires change.

■ Which of the following statements about growth and change do you relate to?
- ☐ Change is not easy for me.
- ☐ Why change? My belief system seems to have worked for me for many years.
- ☐ Certain childhood messages—for example, "The Bible is inerrant," "I am a sinner," "I am a bad person," "Don't question, don't doubt"—are hard to overcome.

- [ ] If I change, someone will be very unhappy or angry with me.
- [ ] I was told not to question or doubt the church, its teaching, or its ministers.
- [ ] If I do question or doubt, something terrible will happen to me.
- [ ] The constant threat that if I doubt or question, then when I die, I will go straight to hell.
- [ ] No one ever gave me permission to doubt or question without severe consequences.
- [ ] If I don't do what the church tells me, I'll be excommunicated.

Let me reassure you, none of the above statements are true. Jesus spent his life questioning and doubting Jewish leadership. See Matthew 23.

SOME SUGGESTIONS ABOUT HOW TO USE THIS BOOK (pp. 74–76)

As you start trying to figure out who or what God is, here are some questions to ponder.

- Do you think God designed the Holocaust? Why or why not?

_____

_____

- How or why did this horrific event happen if God is in charge?

_____

_____

- Do you think God designed your birth, the events in your life, and the date for your death? Why or why not?

_____

_____

- Do you have free will to make your own decisions, or has your entire life been planned down to the minutest detail? Explain your answer.

_____

_____

- Do you believe in predestination? Why or why not?

_____

_____

If you are conflicted as you try to answer these questions, please keep pondering them until you can give a definitive answer to each question. These exercises are simply examples of what needs to happen. The first building block is understanding how the Bible was written. It is extremely important to have this information before moving on.

It is also extremely important for learners to develop a clear understanding of who or what their God is. The image of an old white man living above the third tier of the flat earth in his many mansions is not going to get them very far in the twenty-first century.

Whatever stage you are in, please do not stop praying. Again, understanding how that works in the progressive world involves several steps.

SOME CLOSING THOUGHTS (pp. 76–77)

■ You have finished the workbook. Please share your feelings at this time.

_____

_____

■ Was the workbook helpful? Why or why not?

_____

_____

■ What is your next step?

_____

_____

"Then Do Believe It"[11]

"But if you see in this unbelievable Christmas story
    the man who grew up to show us the meaning of life,
    to reveal the heart of the universe
    and to help us handle the most powerful thing in the world,
    love,
Then do believe it," said Vicar.

"By the way, do you know the Easter story?
Now there's something for you really not to believe!"

SUGGESTED READING

How to Make Love (the Agape kind) with Jesus (2023), by William Aulenbach.

---

[11] Adapted from "Nativity" by Rev. David Keighley in his book *Poems, Piety, and Psyche*, p. 103.

PROGRESSIVE CHRISTIAN RESOURCES

ProgressiveChristianity.org is headquartered in Gig Harbor, Washington. It publishes a weekly newsletter, *Progressing Spirit*, which presents a column by a different progressive clergyperson every week, a Q&A section, and an article by the late Bishop John Shelby Spong. The organization sends out a free weekly email full of Progressive Christian resources. The website also offers a list of progressive churches globally. The organization is completely self-funded.

Westar Institute (http://www.westarinstitute.org) was started in 1985 by noted biblical scholar Robert Funk. The group is composed of over two hundred scholars from many different disciplines: archaeologists, biblical scholars, Old and New Testament professors, church historians, linguists, religious historians, and only a few members of the clergy. The scholars started the Jesus Seminar and have continued studying God, the early church, Paul, and the historical Jesus. Atheists, agnostics, Jews, Christians, Muslims, and people from other religions are involved in the movement. Anyone can join as either a scholar or an interested person. The institute presents workshops around the world. It has a bimonthly newsletter and presents workshops all around the country at least twice a year.

THE POWER OF AGAPE

Unconditional love demands that . . .

Judgment is not allowed. Agape is unconditional and every human is equal.

My prejudices are unacceptable.

A person's skin color is irrelevant.

Your sexual orientation is none of my business.

Gender is a nonissue.

I do not care if you have been in prison, are homeless, have mental challenges, or are in our unjust justice system. You are a fellow human being and deserve to be treated as an equal at all times.

I couldn't care less about how much money or power or influence you have or don't have. I just have to accept you where you are on your life's journey.

A pedophile, mass murderer, mentally challenged person, homeless person, or addict is not who you really are. I need to totally accept you now. If we build trust, maybe you will evolve to become who you really are and share the true you.

My conscience can never be my guide. Agape is.

Forgiveness demands that . . .

I must be willing to forgive you, no matter what your issue is. Forgiveness frees me and allows you to be open so you can move on with your life.

The same goes for me forgiving me, in spite of myself.

Vengeance, retributive "justice," an "eye for an eye and a tooth for a tooth," caging people or executing them are not acceptable to the principle of agape. My role is to try to bring out the best in you.

If certain people harmed society, they should not be locked up in a cage, dehumanized, placed in solitary confinement. They need to be respected for who they could be and then given the tools to learn new ways to do life.

My role is always to move away from the negative and see the glass as half-full.

Not forgiving self or others will eventually kill the real me and waste a lot of my time.

Caring demands that . . .

We respect all Creation. That includes all humans and everything that is living. (But I do have a difficult time respecting critters that try to bite me, such as mosquitoes, snakes, and coyotes.)

We are all caregivers of and for creatures of Creation.

Sometimes caring can be huge; other times it might simply be holding a door open, with a smile.

Caring includes listening attentively, sometimes reacting, mostly just listening.

We care for all people whether we like them or not.

THIS IS AGAPE, THE TOTAL PACKAGE.

To live agape has given me great freedom as well as a peace that passes all understanding. It keeps my life positive and simple. I do not have to make judgments about others, listen to my prejudices, hate anyone or anything, pay attention to the church's theology, get even, or be negative. This frees me to be all that I can be.

Believers in Exile

Rev. David Keighley

I have been forced into exile.
It is not a voluntary action,
but a forced dislocation into an unknown world
with no promise of a safe return
or arrival at some future safe mooring.

Like the Jews, I wonder how I will again
"Sing the Lord's song in a foreign land"?
Like them, I am in exile.
My faith is floundering in a world where
God has gone.
His old meaning lost in this single-tiered universe
with no Heaven for him to hide in
or clouds to cover his face,
as he scatters his Divine interventions.

My faith becomes an irrelevant sidenote
in the light of Christian thinking,
as Newton, Darwin, Freud, and Einstein
enter our consciousness
and shuts God out of our closed existence.
Suddenly he is not out there in the sky after all
to be met after death if we have been good.

As the Jews could not return to the old days and the old ways,
neither can believers in exile pretend
our postmodern world doesn't exist.
We are in exile in a new land
and believers in exile face the death of the old God,
which may not be the death of God at all
but rather an opportunity to ask will he now grow
or die.

(Acknowledgments to Jack Spong for the title.)

Index

ABOUT THE AUTHOR

The Reverend Dr. William H. Aulenbach served as an Episcopal clergyman, pastor, and teacher for several decades. After receiving his master of theology from the Church Divinity School of the Pacific in Berkeley, California, he spent fifteen years in the Diocese of Hawai'i, where he was a rector, a vicar to a Hawaiian congregation, a youth minister to more than 2,500 teenagers, and the founder of a drug clinic, coffeehouse, and runaway shelter. He then returned to California, where he worked in the Diocese of Los Angeles for thirty years as a volunteer or a poorly paid assistant to a rector.

He is the author of several books, including *What's Love Got to Do with It?*, *How to Get to Heaven without Going to Church*, and *Cramming for the Finals*.

He and his wife, Anne, have three daughters and live in Southern California.

For more information about Bil and his books or to sign up to receive his thought-provoking blog, please visit his website, Peace Love Joy Hope (peacelovejoyhope.com).